T0114227

Order this book online at www.trafford.com
or email orders@trafford.com

Most Trafford titles are also available at major online book retailers.

Printed in Victoria, BC, Canada.

ISBN: 978-1-4251-5372-4 (sc)


Our mission is to efficiently provide the world's finest, most comprehensive book publishing
service, enabling every author to experience success. To find out how to publish your book, your
way, and have it available worldwide, visit us online at www.trafford.com

Trafford rev. 3/24/2010

www.trafford.com

North America & international
toll-free: 1 888 232 4444 (USA & Canada)
phone: 250 383 6864 ♦ fax: 812 355 4082

# THE GROWING-UP YEARS

*An Anthology of Short Stories*

*Compiled by MedC Harry*

# Acknowledgements

I have to thank my Almighty God for allowing me to have a determination that hasn't ever quit and the will to persevere.

To all the contributors—you guys and gals are great. Thanks for entrusting me with your works of imagination and experience.

# TABLE OF CONTENTS

## 5     *ALMOST NON-FICTION*

First Real World Encounter→ *by Recee Harry*........7

Just a Little Tap→ *by Omena Ubogu*..................10

The Very First Date→ *by Omena Ubogu*.............18

Purple Wilma→ *by Tanya Browne*....................22

## 30     *MOSTLY FICTION*

A Way to End it All → *by MedC Harry*...............32

CoCooN→ *by MedC Harry*...........................44

Drugs of Revenge→ *by Tanya Browne*................57

Introduction to the Edge→ *by Michael Polack*........69

Daddy's Girl→ *by Abegail Dagdag*....................98

# ALMOST NON-FICTION

*These stories are based on events that have happened in the presence of the author and in some cases to the author him/herself.*

# First Real World Encounter

*By Recee Harry*

I got the job, and I felt like I'd won a trophy. After five years of working in a theme park, I felt as if I'd received a promotion to the real world. I was on my way to my second "real job," minus the costume and the theme park spirit. No more mandatory smiling at all park guests, including the animals. No more wearing an over-sized floppy hat with matching nylons, and best of all, no more comments from new hires, questioning my mental health for having worked at Canada's Wonderland for five seasons.

Maureen, the head beauty advisor, told me that she probably wouldn't have hired me, but since Alanna, my younger sister, worked there she knew I would be just as good. I really didn't want to be reminded that I got the job based on my sister's employment with the company, but Maureen felt the need to mention it. I think the real reason she hired me was because she couldn't find any other suitable candidates. The "Cosmetician Wanted" sign hung at the front of the store for over two months. I was grateful for the job, and I knew I would enjoy being a *beauty advisor*. Anything was better than having to go back to the theme park world. I knew absolutely nothing about makeup and skin cleansers, but I'm a talker; I knew that all I had to do was speak with conviction and the customer would believe me.

After my first week at Shoppers Drug Mart, I began to understand the life of a Shoppers Drug Mart employee and, more importantly, the life a Shoppers Cosmetician. My five-hour shifts were filled with spraying perfumes and cologne on people, stocking nail polish, lipstick and skin cleaners. On a slow night when no orders arrived, my five-hour shift was filled with sweeping in and around the cosmetics area and "facing up" the products on the shelves.

After my first month at Shoppers Drug Mart things became much more eventful. I joined the PTS (part-time students). We were the group of part-time workers by night and full-time university or college students by day. We arrived at work a half an hour before our shift to get caught up on the latest store events. The events ranged from community happenings to what was happening in the lives of the adult full-timers. The information got passed down from the alumni PTS members—past part-timers now working in the store full time after graduating from university. It was through this group that I learned the store had a big problem with shoplifters, prostitutes, heroin and crack-cocaine addicts, and alcoholics. Angelo, the floorwalker, told me that if I ever needed security, I was to use the public address system and ask for a head cashier to *Aisle Eleven*. (The store only had eight aisles.)

I felt grateful for the tips because for every one of my shifts in July, the same prostitute came in our store at nine o'clock to put on her makeup using our testers. She knew exactly what colours she wanted and where to find them. I never bothered her; I figured she wasn't doing anything wrong—really. Also in July, Marty, the biggest coke addict in the community, walked into the store. He was about 5 feet 7 inches tall; he wore a knitted cap in the middle of July, and sang and danced to a song that only he seemed to hear. He first staggered down the baby aisle and picked up a jar of petroleum jelly, and then he picked up a can of air freshener, and finally a pack of AA batteries. After completing his shopping, he walked right out of the store, ignoring the blaring alarm system and the four employees who tried to stop him. My customer service experience came from a friendly theme park, so I refused to believe that he didn't pay for his goods.

The Saga in the World of "Shoplifters Drug Mart" continued, and I decided that I would do my part to help my employer with some of the store's problems. That's when I noticed Peter the Panhandler-Alcoholic coming into the store. I quickly cleared all the rubbing alcohol off the shelves. This worked for both of us: he would have to drink his coke minus the rubbing alcohol, and I wouldn't have to take a handful of wet dimes, nickels and pennies from him.

Then Gertrude the Gravol Thief came in. I tried to follow her so she would have trouble stealing the pills. I still don't know how a woman in her seventies could be so quick. I usually succeeded in deterring her, but once I had to stop to spray cologne on a *wom-man* (to this day I still don't exactly know if Terrie is male or female), so I couldn't follow Gertrude. She took the little pink tablets out of the box and threw the box in the bin with the cosmetic bags.

She was messing in the wrong section—I took pride in my work area. As old Gerty stood looking at liquid foundation, I picked up the empty box and said out loud to the row of liquid foundations, "Oh, I wonder how this got here. I just tidied this aisle and it wasn't here before. Oh, well." I picked up the loud speaker and said in a thunderous voice of authority, "Security to Cosmetics please. Security to Cosmetics."

Now, any good Shoppers Drug Mart shoplifter knew that we never called security by actually using the word "security," but old Gerty wasn't a good shoplifter. Before anyone had a chance to get to the cosmetics area, old Gerty limped to my counter. With a blend of mascara and tears rolling down her drooping, wrinkled cheeks, Gerty explained that she took the Gravol out of the box because she didn't have her glasses and couldn't read the package. She didn't mention how or why the pills were tucked away in the bottom of her bag, right next to her bingo markers. But that didn't matter, because I taught old Gerty a lesson in messing with *this* night beauty advisor.

# Just a Little Tap
*By Omena Ubogu*

"Tunde, your principal is on the phone," my mother shouted.

My heart raced faster as I quickly got off my bed and slipped my feet into my slippers. It was weird; I was simultaneously dragging my feet and quickening my pace as I moved to the living room. On one level, I wanted to hear what he was going to say, to know what the next chapter in the saga was going to be, and on the other, I was scared to hear what he had to say. Maybe if I'd been a different type of person I wouldn't have been in such a mess.

Wednesday, March 10th began like every other day. The rest of the school had gone back to the dorms after afternoon prep, but like always, I stayed behind to finish up my assignments. My Integrated Science homework was a little more difficult than I'd anticipated, so I needed some water to cool off. The walk to the tap had put a little strain on my wounded leg, so I leaned against a wall for a quick rest. That was when I looked across and saw a group of senior boys laughing and kicking something in the sand.

❧

"About this matter with Chike..." Principal Okorie continued.

Yes, Chike. It was the first day of Form One and as I was unpacking my trunk, a skinny dark-skinned boy bent over and picked something out of my bag.

"What's this?" he asked, looking down at me.

"Garlic."

He crinkled his nose. "For what?"

"My asthma. My doctor said I should take it."

"As in, eat it raw?"

I nodded.

He threw it back into the bag and laughed. "Pele o."

And thus began our friendship. Even though we weren't in the same form, the fact that his bunk was about ten feet from mine meant that I saw him every day. As most boys normally did, we wrestled and played, so it wasn't particularly odd when about two months earlier, he brought out the two carving knives he had stolen from the school kitchen and asked me to fight "kung-fu" with him.

The events still remain sketchy, but all that I remember was that one moment: I was listening to the sound of clanging metal, and next, his knife was deep in my thigh. It was one of those surreal moments when I didn't even feel one ounce of pain, till I looked at my thigh and could only see the handle.

As some of the other boys carried me out of my room—my leg leaving a red trail—I looked into Chike's begging eyes and realized that I needed to be a true friend. So when I later got questioned by the school authorities, I maintained that I mistakenly stabbed myself with a knife I'd stolen. They were skeptical about my tale, but I didn't budge, so they had no choice but to accept my story and punish me. I realized they were being very lenient by only sentencing me to spend every Saturday till the end of the term cutting grass or pounding clogged toilets, but I realized that it was much better than having Chike suspended, or worse, expelled so close to our JSSCEs.

❧

He cleared his throat and continued, "As I told you, Tunde, we only wanted to get to the bottom of it. All we needed was confirmation."

Because unfortunately, my word would never have been good enough—not that I'd believed otherwise on that afternoon of March 11th, when the assistant head boy interrupted my lunch of Pako flakes to inform me that I was being summoned by the principal.

He left me at the door of the building, and I walked in to see that the principal's secretary was away from her desk. I hesitantly knocked at the door and waited for his answer. After hearing his response, I walked in to see five boys kneeling by a wall.

"Tunde, why don't you sit down," he ordered before I could properly digest the scene in front of me. "Do you recognize these boys?"

I nodded.

"From where?"

"I have seen them around the school."

"Anywhere else?"

I knew ratting out my seniors would be tantamount to suicide, so I shook my head. He slowly stood up and walked from behind the desk.

"So why did they identify you?"

My mouth fell open. "Me, sir, as what?"

"As one of them—they say that you also attacked Chike."

My tongue suddenly felt heavy. I swallowed hard. "It's not true, sir. I don't even know them. Why would I do that? I was the one that took him to the sick bay. Chike is my friend," I said quickly, not bothering to take a moment to breathe.

"So are you saying these boys are lying?"

I looked at their hard faces and said, "Please sir, I didn't do anything."

He leaned against the desk. "I see. Why don't you tell me what happened?"

I took a deep breath and gave him the details.

৯

"As you know, as one of our top students," his voice crackled from the other side of the phone, "I only wish the best for you."

I had to do everything in my power to keep from scoffing. Wish the best for me? Yeah, right.

If I were to describe myself, I'd say that I was someone who loved a good challenge. It's not that I loved school, but I saw it for what it was and did my best to conquer it. The same went for sports. Some said the high came from participating, but for me the aim of the game was to win. And I loved every single minute of it. I found that I was athletic, and made sure that, by my JSS2, I was winning every short distance race in the junior category. If the rules could have been bent, I would have loved to beat the seniors too. It wasn't even about getting the prizes—as they were always something pointless, like a book on Calabar art—but about knowing that I was the best, and no drug-induced high could ever make me feel as good.

And that was what made Linda Okorie so appealing.

Sure, I wasn't the only one that noticed her walk in and out of her father's house in her blue checkered blouse and solid blue skirt. And sure, I wasn't the only person that saw that even though she was a little plump, she had a pretty mouth. But I knew I was definitely the only junior boy that had the guts to approach her.

It hadn't been easy dodging the school prefects as I tried to hang around the staff quarters every evening. But my persistence paid off, and eventually she ran into me.

It had been a Thursday evening, and even though it was still sunny, the air was a little cooler, as Harmattan was around the corner. I was getting ready to go to the Dining Hall for dinner when I heard the rustling of feet behind me. I turned around to see her staring at me.

"What are you doing here?" she asked, her lips twisted in a smirk.

With the most poker face I could manage I said, "I am looking for Mrs. Ojo's house."

"Oh..." she lifted her brow. "I think it's two houses behind that one." She pointed to the third house on the left.

"Okay, thank you," I replied, looking over, then lowering my eyes. After another glance at her, I reluctantly turned around.

"Hey, are you all right?" she called.

I hid a smile and turned back around. "Yes. Mrs. Ojo is my family friend and I just wanted to know if there was any news about my mother."

"Your mother? What's wrong with her?"

"She's…" I didn't know what disease to pick as I was a little superstitious and didn't actually want it to befall her. "… not feeling well."

"I'm sorry to hear that," her forehead creased in worry. "Do you want to come in and use the phone here? You can call your house."

But before long, she wasn't much of a challenge—all I needed to do was add two years to my age and tell her all the things she wanted to hear. Soon after, the thrill came from finding a way to always be at her place without getting caught. But, as expected, the inevitable day arrived when her father walked in with some Christmas decorations and saw my hand up his daughter's blouse. At that moment, I realized that a new challenge had arisen—he'd try to find a way of punishing me without exposing her. So I really wasn't surprised when I was called back to the principal's office later that afternoon.

I sat in the waiting room, watching the principal's secretary paint her nails with an artist's precision. I sat still, trying my best to look confident and unaffected even though inside, all I could think about was what the principal had in store for me.

At around 4:30 the secretary gave me the go-ahead.

I pushed open the door to find my frowning father sitting across from the principal. He stood up as I walked into the room.

"Tunde, as I told your father, you are on indefinite suspension starting from today. Go to your room, pack your bags and come back here."

What? I wasn't sure I could trust my ears.

My father nodded and said, "Son, go and get your things."

I stared at him then turned to the principal. "But excuse me sir, I didn't do anything—ask Chike."

"As you know, Chike doesn't remember you being there, but the other boys insist that you only kicked him when he was unconscious."

"Why would I do such a thing, sir? He is my friend!"

"Well, till we get to the bottom of this, you have to go home."

Not knowing what else to do, I got on my knees. "Please sir, I swear, I am innocent, I didn't do it. Chike is my friend, why would I hit him? They are just lying on me!"

"Well, for now, you have to go home. We cannot tolerate this type of nonsense here. If you are telling the truth, it will come out sooner or later. But for now, my hands are tied."

❦

"Anyway, everything has been taken care of and you can come back to school."

For the first time in a week, I breathed easily. "Thank you, thank you, sir."

"There's no need to thank me. Several students came forward and confirmed your story. They all admitted to seeing all the other boys kicking him, but no one remembered seeing you. The other boys have been expelled."

"I see, sir."

"As I told you, the truth will come out, and now we know you were not involved." He sounded a little disappointed.

"I see, sir. When should I return?"

"Since it's already Thursday, why don't you return on Saturday so that you can have time to catch up with your notes?"

"Thank you, sir."

❦

I'd barely waved my parents off when I turned around and ran to Chike's room. "Ol boy, how you dey now?" I asked, taping him on the arm. He was sitting on the lower bunk, looking into his locker.

He looked up at me. "How, now?"

"Shey everything is okay?" His face was still slightly bruised but otherwise, he looked fine.

He nodded then stood up to face me.

"Anyway, abeg I need to borrow your physics notes. Men, I have so much copying to do and Mocks are in two weeks. And you know I must pass. In fact, add biology to that too," I said smiling.

Wordlessly, he turned around, pulled his bag from behind his locker, found the two notebooks and held them out to me.

"Tunde, everything is balanced now, abi?"

Still smiling, I grabbing on to the books. "Heh?"

He held on to the books and looked into my eyes. "I said it's finished. You don't owe me anything and I don't owe you anything. Okay?"

I nodded slowly. I hadn't realized that he'd known all along.

✎

It really had begun like any other day. The walk to the tap had put a little strain on my healing leg, so I leaned against a wall for a quick rest. I was looking around when I saw a group of boys kicking something in the sand. I immediately turned my face and started to leave when I heard someone call my name. I turned around to see a senior boy in his white crisp trousers, gesturing for me to go to him.

"Do you know this boy?" The rest of his friends stopped kicking and backed away so that I could see his face.

I barely recognized Chike underneath the blood. I shook my head vehemently.

"Why are you lying?"

"Senior Ahmed, I am not lying." He was the only one in Yellow House with us.

"Really? Then how come I always see you together?"

My lower lip quivered. "I…I don't know."

"This isn't your friend?"

I shook my head again.

"Then prove it," said the yellow-skinned, Igbo-looking boy at the other end.

"How?"

"Like this." He kicked him.

"But…but, he didn't do anything to me."

"And so? If you don't know him, you will kick him."

"But…"

"Are you deaf? Kick him or face punishment."

From the looks on their faces, I knew that if I didn't comply I'd face the same fate Chike had. Maybe it was a challenge I should have attempted to conquer, but at that moment all I could see was Chike's swollen face. So I chose to give him a little tap. But the pain in my right leg made it difficult to lift it high. Then I looked down at his face and saw the source of that pain—the reason I'd missed a lot of classes, the reason I would not be competing in the Interhouse sports or even in the football match against our biggest rivals, and as I thought of this, the soft tap transformed into a succession of hard kicks, and I just kept kicking till their robust laughs permeated my anger.

My body went still. With an uneven mix of shame and relief, I looked from their animated faces to his lifeless body and slowly limped away.

# The Very First Date
*By Omena Ubogu*

"You're making that up! There's no way that happened!" I was cackling like a hyena.

"It sure did," he said, his eyebrows moving excitedly.

I sipped wine as he shared the details of his latest anecdote. Anyone watching us at the restaurant would never have guessed we were on a first date.

Last Saturday, I dragged my two best friends, Laura and Julia, to an African Students Association event. Thirty minutes into it, as we were devising a plan to discreetly leave, Julia spotted him. He was about 6 feet 3, light skinned, toned like a male model and owned a smile that could melt the North Pole. After twenty minutes of intense staring, a few arguments, followed by a few rounds of "rock, paper, scissors," Julia won the opportunity to approach him.

So you can imagine my surprise when, shortly after, a frowning Julia returned with him in tow and introduced us. Ten minutes later, Moke and I separated ourselves from the group and spent the rest of the evening as a twosome.

For a week, I'd wondered why he'd picked me over my friend, so I asked.

"You don't like that I came to talk to you instead?"

"No. That's not it. It's just that she's so beautiful. All the guys always go for her. I'm just wondering why you didn't."

He was nodding his head. "Yes, she is beautiful, but so are you. In fact I find you more attractive."

I blushed. "Really?"

He looked at me like I was crazy. "Of course, don't you see that?"

"I guess so." I really didn't know how to respond. "So you came to talk to me because you thought I was more beautiful?" I figured I'd milk it because, well...why not?

"Yes...no...I don't know. I just had a feeling about you. Like I knew you or something. Actually, more like you were someone I should know. So I went with that. And I'm glad I did. Aren't you?"

"What do you think?"

We spent the rest of the evening talking and flirting shamelessly, and if the restaurant didn't have to close, we would have stayed there till daybreak because neither of us paid any attention to the time.

On the ride home I couldn't help but be tickled by the entire situation. All my life I'd dealt with useless, unsupportive, uncaring, selfish leeches and like a dream, he'd stepped into my life.

As we walked to the entrance door of my dormitory, I looked at him and said, "So..."

"So, did you have a great time?" he said through smiling lips.

"Of course I did. Can't you tell?" I giggled hoping he didn't recognize that it was a ruse to mask raging nerves.

"Would I be jumping to conclusions by assuming that means you'd like to do this again?"

"Well, that depends. Did you have a good time? And would you like to do this again?" I teased, looking into his eyes.

He looked back into mine and before I knew it, I was putting my hands on the back of his neck and pulling his face dangerously close to mine.

"What do you think?" he asked sexily, as his hands slipped to the small of my back and he pulled my body to his. Before I could respond, I felt his soft lips imploring mine. Slowly and surely my brains turned into mush. He expertly and passionately kissed me in such a playful and very romantic fashion that I found myself matching his every move. We spent about five minutes stuck like glue before we heard the church bells chime twelve times. I broke away from him as I was jolted back into reality. However, I noticed that my actions confused him.

"Remember, I have my church thing tomorrow?" I explained.

"I would suggest you ditch, but I don't want to find myself mysteriously struck by lightning on the way home."

"No, that wouldn't be good." We laughed.

"So," he said, clapping his hands, "we've not actually solidified any plans. What should we do next? I would say a dinner and a movie, but look what happened today." We had planned to see a movie after our dinner.

I thought about it. "Well, there's a movie I really wanna see, so maybe we'll see the movie first next time?" We were both grinning like fools. "How about next Friday?"

He softly caressed my face. "But Friday seems so far away."

"That's why telephones were invented. You can always call me."

He groaned. "Yeah, but I want to see you before then."

"How about after my meeting tomorrow? We are usually done by noon. So what about lunch at...at about one?" I stammered because his alluring eyes were working wonders on my psyche.

He pulled my face close to his as he kissed my lips. "It's a date."

I turned to leave but changed my mind. A nagging question had been on my mind for the past week, so I chose to satisfy my curiosity.

"Moke, can I ask you a question?" I asked sheepishly.

"Sure, what?"

"Well, it's your name. It's rather unique. Where did you get it from?"

"It's Nigerian—it's short for Emamoke."

I groaned.

He looked concerned and touched my arm. "Are you okay?"

I smiled wearily. "Yeah, I'm fine. It's just that that name brings back awful memories. I'm glad I don't have to call you by it."

His interest was piqued. "Aww, but how could my full name bring back such awful memories? I don't get that."

I shrugged my shoulders dismissively. "Just this idiot I met in the summer of '87 when I was on holidays visiting my grandma in Nigeria. I mean—"

"I didn't know you were from Africa," he interjected.

"Well, my parents are." He kept staring. "Anyway, this boy called Emamoke Umukoro—I shall never forget that name—he tormented my life the whole stay. He called me names, chased after me, threw things and just made my stay rather memorable—and not in a good way."

I couldn't understand what happened, but suddenly he could barely keep himself from laughing.

"Go on," he implored.

I giggled nervously. "That's pretty much it. I swore that if I every saw him again I would punch his lights out—stupid ninny."

He leaned toward me then put his hands behind his back. "All right then, take your best shot."

Confused and suspicious I asked, "Excuse me?"

He laughed and stretched out his hand. "I think I need to re-introduce myself to you." With an exaggerated bow he said, "I am your tormentor—Mr. Emamoke Umukoro."

I was really confused. "No...no..." I couldn't believe it. "It can't be."

He kept nodding his head. "I'm afraid it is."

"But, but, but your name..."

"Yeah...my Father changed it in '88, after we moved to the States," he said with dancing eyes.

With a frown I stared at him for about a minute. As if on cue, we both burst into a fit of hysterics.

# Purple Wilma
*By Tanya Browne*

"Mmm…this is good." I hummed to myself as I regretfully chewed and swallowed the last purple Wilma Flinstone vitamin, for that was when I knew it was my last one. As I finished, I let out a loud "burp" and looked at the empty bottle sitting on the bed. Mom's going to kill me, I thought to myself as I walked towards the empty bottle. I picked up the bottle and fumbled with the lid as I attempted to screw it back on. The lid then rolled under the bed. I frantically looked for it and saw it next to three vitamins I guess I had dropped earlier. I looked at the vitamins with excitement and was tempted to eat them; however, at the same time I was disappointed because I knew if I ate them, my mother would surely know what I had done. I sadly placed the orange Barney, orange Pebbles and purple Wilma back into the empty bottle and screwed on the lid. I then took the close to empty bottle into my wobbly hands and placed it back on the spot it always occupied on the chest.

"Maybe she won't notice," I said softly to myself as I walked to the door and unlocked it, closing it behind me. It was now time for me to get ready for bed.

The next morning had come fairly quickly. I didn't get that much sleep the night before. I was sweating, and kept tossing and turning. When I was ready to get out of bed, I couldn't.

"DADDY!" I yelled so loud that my bedroom windows started to shake. He came running in like a bull charging at a red flag.

"What! What's wrong?" he said, with his blue eyes looking wildly around the room to see what was the problem.

"I can't move my legs," I said as tears started to fill my eyes and my voice started to shake. He helped me out of bed and helped me stand. I started to walk again. I was so happy when I took my first steps, like an infant taking theirs.

When I went downstairs, my aunt was sitting in the living room. I tried to avoid her because I didn't want to talk to her. She always came by our house on the weekends. I never understood why because we saw her every day. She lived in a big house that was a couple of houses away from ours. It was a scary-looking house, and it gave people an eerie feeling as they passed by. The little kids on the block said that a witch lived there, but I never told them it was my aunt.

On weekdays my mother would bring my baby brother to her house while my sister and I went there after school so she could take care of us. More like I would take care of them. I never wanted to go to her house because I didn't like her, she pretended too much. I spent most of my time alone in her house going off into little adventures to keep myself occupied until my parents came to pick us up. My aunt was a skinny and tall woman who wore big thick square glasses that had dark rims. Her hair had been in braids ever since last fall, and it had an awful stench to it.

In the afternoon I had another craving for the Flinstone vitamins, so I had asked my mother if I could have one. I was so sure she wouldn't notice the almost empty bottle I had left on the chest in her room the night before. She went up the stairs and I marched behind her like I was a soldier following my lieutenant. She went into her room and I skipped behind her. I was like a child on Christmas morning, anxious and excited, waiting to open a present.

Her arm jumped up to grab the bottle, like a predator attacking its prey. As soon as she lifted up the bottle, she shrieked, "Chris!"

My father then came running up the stairs and busted into the room.

"Rachel! What happened?"

"The vitamin bottle is empty."

She then unscrewed the top and pulled out the cotton inside, showing him the three vitamins that were left behind. My parents automatically looked at me. They knew right away that I was the culprit because my brother was just a baby and my sister was too good to do such a thing. I was immediately put on the witness stand and cross-examined. That was something my father did best. He was a criminal lawyer and had a way of asking people questions. He worked most of the time and very rarely spent his weekends at home. My mother, on the other hand, was a high school teacher and had a harsh way of talking to people. She rarely smiled or showed any emotion toward us.

"Did you do this?" my mother asked as if she didn't know.

"Yes I did," I said with a smile on my face, happy to hear their concern.

"When did you eat it? And why?" my father then asked.

I told them what they wanted to know, and I felt good inside because I knew they really cared.

My parents immediately told me to get dressed because I had to go to the hospital.

My father stayed home with my brother and sister while my mother, aunt and I went to the hospital. We had to take the bus because our car was in the shop and my aunt didn't have one. I remember the bus ride. It was long and boring. My mother and aunt were talking, and I remember resenting the fact that my aunt came with us. I felt as though it was supposed to be our time together, and the pretender had invited herself. She was ruining the moment my mother and I were supposed to have together. We sat in the horizontal aisle window seats facing the driver, and I sat like a crushed Raggedy Ann doll, in-between my mother and aunt.

The bus smelled like gas fumes mixed with food and the horrible stench of my aunt's year-old braids. The seats were blue and soft, and hardly anyone occupied them. There was a man sitting right across from us and all by himself. A woman and a man were sitting way in the back of the bus; a couple of old people were sitting in the side seats, and a little boy with a young man, either his father or older brother. I focused on them immediately.

The little boy looked about five, which was three years younger than me. He was laughing and making truck sounds as he drove his toy truck along the back of the seat in front of him. The man he was with kept looking at him and smiling. He then reached into his pocket and pulled out a candy, giving it to the little boy. The boy smiled and said thank-you as the man reached down and kissed the child on his forehead. A while later, the man reached up and pulled the string that rang the bell for them to get off. As they got up, I watched them exit the doors when the bus came to a complete stop. I leaned across my mother as I pressed my face against the window, watching them walk away in the colourful, crispy leaves as the bus started to drive off. I only felt one thing. Envy. The little boy had it all.

I sat back in my spot, quietly watching the cars go by. I then found myself counting how many blue cars I saw. One, two…three…four, five, six…. I was suddenly interrupted by an arm around my shoulders. I turned my head towards the window to see if it was my mother, but with great disappointment I found out it wasn't. It was my aunt. She looked at me with a half smile, as her thick glasses pressed against her big nose.

"Are you okay?"

I nodded my head as she said something else. I couldn't quite hear her; it was just mumbles to me. My vision was blurry every once in a while and my hearing seemed to be going on and off. With annoyance, I turned my head towards the window and looked for blue cars to count. There were none. The bus suddenly turned into a long narrow street with cars parked on both sides. There was a tall grey building on the left side of the street. Ambulance trucks were near the emergency entrance and people were walking in and out of the building. Some people were in wheelchairs and others used crutches. The bell suddenly rang; it was my mother who pulled it. It was now time for us to get off the bus. We were finally there. We were at the hospital.

The emergency room was full of people who had all sorts of injures. We walked up to the front desk and told the receptionist what the problem was. We gave her the health card and the answers to the information she needed to know. We then took a seat and waited to be called in.

The seats were dark blue with cushions on them. My aunt sat beside me, with my mother beside her. The room smelt like dry blood and ten-day-old medication. There were children crying and men and women screaming in pain. Sitting on my left side was a man who had bloodstains on his yellow sweatshirt and a bloody face. He kept using his left hand to tend to his right eye, dabbing it with a bloody cloth while his right hand stayed limp on his lap. He looked like he'd been in a fight, or maybe a car accident.

"Mr. Gravis?" a woman dressed in a white dress called out. She was standing in the doorway where the patients went to get the care they needed. She was in her mid-thirties and had dark brown hair, long like my mother's. She had a clipboard with her and looked at it as she called out the name again. "Mr. Gravis, the doctor is ready to see you," she looked around with uncertainty, as if she hadn't said the name correctly.

Immediately, the man sitting beside me jumped up and walked towards the woman. She stretched out her arm and cradled it around his back, leading him into the doorway. "Sir, you're going to be just fine."

As I watched him enter the room, I noticed a bloody cloth sitting on the sparkling white floor of the emergency room. The man that was sitting beside me must have dropped it when he got up. A woman limped into the room, dragging the bloody cloth across the floor as she went to the front desk to ask for assistance. A thick streak of maroon was left across the floor, ruining the beautiful finish it had.

I looked at the pale green walls and noticed funny little cartoons hanging on it. I guess they were there to cheer people up. On a little table in the corner of the room there were pamphlets and health magazines. I was suddenly called next, and my mother came with me as my aunt stayed behind. I was brought into a room that had a bed covered with a light blue sheet. The doctor was a thin

Chinese man, tall and lanky like a giraffe's neck. He wore a long white lab coat, dark grey pants underneath and black shoes.

"Hello there," he said as he kindly guided me towards the examination bed. He turned around and asked my mother what had happened to me, and with disappointment she told him what I had done. He told me to sit still while he examined me.

"Does this hurt?" he said as he pressed in my stomach.

"No," I lied. I did feel pain, and I had been feeling it ever since I ate those vitamins. I had also been feeling pretty dizzy, but I never said a word.

"Are you sure?"

"Yes," I claimed.

He then brought me to the x-ray room to check my stomach. He couldn't see a thing. The vitamins were already on their way to be digested. He brought me back and spoke to my mother. I looked at her as she sat sternly in the wooden chair.

"It's too late for me to pump her stomach. There is no trace of the vitamins."

"Well, is there anything you could do?"

"No! But there is nothing for you to be worried about. Just make sure she doesn't eat any more of those vitamins."

He slowly turned around and moved towards his drawer. He opened it and pulled out a lollipop, holding it in front of my face.

"You're lucky you know, you could have died. Make sure you stay away from those vitamins." He handed me the lollipop and smiled.

"Thank you!" I said with a big smile on my face.

My mother and I left the doctor's office and went out into the waiting room.

My aunt jumped out of her chair. "Is everything okay?"

"Yes," my mother said, holding back her tears, not wanting us to see her cry, "she's going to be just fine."

She put her arms around me and gave me a big hug, and a tear dropped on my forehead when she pulled away. I was surprised. The last time my mother cried was when her father died of a heart attack. Ever since that day of the funeral, my mother hadn't been the same. She never cried about anything. She really did care, and that made me feel good inside. I felt just as lucky as the boy I had seen on the bus. My mother called my father and told him the good news. I was going to be okay. We then went outside, ready to catch the next bus.

Around 8:30 p.m. we got home and my aunt returned to her house. It was already dark and it had started snowing. My father greeted us at the door with the warm heat of the house. He stretched out his arms and gave me a big hug and kiss.

"I knew you would be all right," he said with tears filling his eyes.

I was ecstatic. I felt a warm feeling in my heart. I had not felt that in a long time. After the big moment, I went upstairs with a huge smile on my face. I felt good. As I was ready to enter the small room my sister and I shared, my mother called out.

"Bring me my briefcase."

"Okay," I yelled back.

I entered my parent's room and walked over to the night table on the other side of the bed next to the window. I picked up the briefcase that was beside it and looked out the window with my blurry vision. Big flakes were falling out of the sky and a misty light surrounded each one as they quickly hit the ground.

"Did you find it?" my mother yelled out.

"Yes! I'm coming."

I turned away from the window and let the long pink curtains fall back. I turned around and saw the bottle of vitamins, sitting on its spot on the chest. I had a sudden craving for it and remembered the three I had left inside.

Not remembering anything the doctor had said, I placed my mother's briefcase on the bed and stumbled across the room toward the chest. I then reached up to get the vitamin bottle. I opened the bottle and ate orange Barney and orange Pebbles and looked at my favourite purple Wilma vitamin sitting in the palm of my hand. I motioned to pop it into my mouth and felt a sudden pain in my chest. I dropped the vitamin and clenched my chest. In the background, I could hear my parents calling my name. I wanted to answer, but the pain was so great. I was choking on my words.

I suddenly hit the beige carpet in my parents' room and, in the distance, I could hear running. My parents. I looked straight ahead and saw their feet. I heard the wailing of my mother, a sound that I had never heard before. All that was left was the lonely, unforgettable cries of my parents and the sound of silence. I was gone, and the last thing I had seen was a large purple light. It was my purple Wilma, and it was bringing me on my way to heaven.

# MOSTLY FICTION

*Each of these stories were created in the imagination and sprinkled with a few real-life events.*

# A Way to End it All
*By MedC Harry*

Preteenhood entered my life; it was a breeze, right! The first event that I, Grega Canster, wanted to be a part of was…boys. Of course it wasn't easy, mainly because mom and dad were not having it. They made it clear: "After your education you can go find anyone you want!" This was starting out to be a really difficult task because boys were allergic to me. I knew it wasn't all of them; it was only the ones that I had met. Luckily, I had my constant companion, my notepad. I turned to it for guidance, in search of why boys didn't like me but loved Luanne.

Luanne had light back-length hair, long lashes that were darker than her hair and never-ending legs. She never did homework, but she got great grades and played the best dodgeball I had ever seen a girl play. Although she had so many positive attributes, she didn't show off. She embraced everyone equally, especially the girls who were not popular.

I, on the other hand, was the opposite of Luanne. I had short hair, short lashes, short legs and long arms. Was not even a little bit outgoing, could serve a mean volleyball, but don't let that ball come over the net to visit because I would run, no bumping for me, just running, while hoping that the ball wouldn't hit me. Forget dodgeball, I was always the second last to be picked for a team, unless of course Luanne was the captain, then I would be the first to be picked and the third to get tagged and sit out of the game.

Luanne got all the attention and didn't care. People would walk up to her requesting to touch her long locs; others would stand and give her the stare of death, and Luanne would go up to them and start a conversation. She had such a positive spirit.

I had no spirit at all. I was the one to stand on the sidelines, knowing that people were watching and perhaps commenting on my low desire to mingle. But, oh well. I wasn't the hang-out type; no parties, no amusement parks, no touch tag, no camping trips, just leave me alone and I was happy.

Honestly, I wasn't always that way. I remember the day I changed. It was Sunday, April 17, 1992. I sat in my bedroom wondering what life was all about. I wasn't thirteen yet. Although I had a close to perfect life, I didn't want it. I made a decision: sixteen would not see me alive. My parents got to choose me, but they didn't care how I felt. Suppose I didn't want them as parents, or suppose I wasn't ready to come to earth until the 21st century? I made my decision; I would take my exit before April 20, 1996. I was not sure how my swan song would be performed, but I was sure I would make it as simple as possible. I resolved to live out loud before that day arrived.

I was always being dragged somewhere. If it wasn't church, it was an awful picnic, if not a picnic, someone's house, if not there, somewhere else where I would rather not be. My dragging days were brutal, but my focus remained intact: At sixteen, I was outta here. I didn't like people, so there was no point in sticking around to meet more of them. Nobody was worth my time. Not my brother, not my sister, not dad, not mom.

I had a few friends, well, two to be exact: Pebulla and Luanne. We all knew each other, but Luanne and Pebulla were not as close as I was to each of them. Luanne was that girl that you could always count on and always have fun with. No matter what the weather or occasion, Luanne was there. Pebulla was that "Plan B" girl; if there was no one else to hangout with, call on Pebulla.

Luanne was so hyper all the time. When I wanted to participate in my Pity Party, Luanne wouldn't let me. She got my spirit going so much that I forgot about my party. We went to the mall for the first time alone when we were thirteen. Each mall event was an adventure with Luanne. I could never be sure whether we would be held for shoplifting or for creating a public nuisance. Luanne would decide once we got there.

My first clue that shopping to Luanne didn't involve money was when we went to The Dollar Change. Luanne opened a bag of Totally Radd Cheddar chips, those were her favourite kinds. She devoured those suckers in less than a minute. You should have seen her go. Once the bag was empty, she went to the teenager at the register.

Luanne said, "Dude, drop dis na man!"

Stu, per his name tag, looked at her then said, "Pardon me?"

"Dash 'em way," Luanne said while staring at Stu with a glazed look in her eyes.

Then I thought it was smart to intervene. "Can you throw that in the garbage for her?"

He did. I saw the confusion in Stu's face. I was hoping Stu didn't notice my disbelief.

I followed Luanne out of the store. "Luanne, do you do that a lot?" I asked.

"Do what?"

"Never mind, never mind!"

As we walked through the mall, I began to question my memory. Maybe she paid and I just didn't notice…or maybe not. Oh, well.

That year, I turned fourteen. I was an old-looking fourteen, so I began to look for a job. I had two years to save and buy all the material things that an average-looking girl without a boyfriend would ever need to remain happy.

The only company that would give me a chance was a telemarketing company. They didn't ask me for my age, so I didn't give it to them. I am sure it wouldn't have mattered much anyway. The place was on the bottom floor of a four-storey apartment building. For each phone number dialed, the floorwalker would be crossing his fingers, hoping that the line was not intercepted. His finger crossing would work for us, sometimes. My job was to call residences to find out if they were interested in donating clothing to charity. That was the year that I learned my first Italian words, *roba vecchio*. I worked there long enough to buy myself an automatic camera.

I moved on after Luanne convinced me that working there was not the way to go. Anything that I wanted she assured me that she could get it for me. I started to believe her when I saw her with a pencil skirt that looked so much like the one my dad bought for me. She got hers around the same time mine went missing. After searching everywhere possible for my skirt, I told Luanne that I lost it. She said, "I can get another one for you, if you want." I begged her not to and told her it just wouldn't be the same.

The real reason was because I was afraid that she would take it from a store by putting it on and walking out. I imagined the entire thing: The sensor would go off and Luanne would take off, running through the mall, hands flailing, eyes bulging out while yelling something crazy like "The man is going to kill me" or "The train is coming"—something that would guarantee her an audience and perhaps force the store owners to believe that she was a whack job not worth chasing for a pencil skirt that was last fall's fashion trend.

Luanne certainly was a character. One Friday we went to Attires, a huge department store. I fell in love with a pair of flip-flops. They were silver with black sequins around the big toe and purple beads lining the outside. They might sound hideous, but they really were cute. I looked at them for a while. I didn't have clothing money on me, just candy money. So I walked away. I forgot to look at the price, so I went back. Then I remembered that dad always felt the bottom of shoes before he bought them and he would make a comment like "Oh good, they're rubber, they'll do." Or "No grip, no go."

I went back so that I could see and feel the grip at the bottom, but when I got there, in the three seconds since I was last there, my love was gone. The cute, sequined flip-flops had disappeared. I searched for a while before coming to terms with the reality that my feet were big and the big sizes usually disappear first. I hadn't seen any customers in the area to follow in an attempt to sway them to give me the shoes. There wasn't a salesperson in sight. Oh well, I thought, I'll just have to annoy my dad so much that he'll take me to the next town over to get those flip-flops.

After I came to grips with my loss, I went searching for Luanne. I found her in the toy department. She was riding a bike with a banana seat. I sat and mourned the loss of my flips-flops while waiting for Luanne to complete her fun day in Attires. I bought a pack of sour gum before leaving the store. I always felt weird leaving stores without buying anything.

We walked around some more before going to the bus stop to catch the bus for home. Luanne lived about a block away from me, which meant she got off the bus one stop before I did. She rang the bell and stood by the door. Just before she stepped down to get off the bus she pulled a stapled yellow paper bag out of her knapsack. She threw it on my lap and said goodbye. I was a lot more than scared to open the grocery bag. So I didn't, right then. Instead, I waited until I got off the bus. I thought about my day while walking up the path that led to my house. With the bag in hand, I sat on my porch for a minute, thinking, is it smart to open this bag?

Well, curiousity got the best of me, so I opened it. My first reaction was to throw it on the ground, after I saw my beloved flip-flops and two packs of sour gum. I was scared and happy at the same time. I loved the shoes, but I hated that they weren't purchased in front of me.

Luanne had already called, my mom told me. I knew that I wasn't going to call her back right then; but I didn't know if I was going to call her during that week, and if I did, I wouldn't know what I would say. She called three more times while I was inside, but I was busy each time, and if I wasn't I would have made myself busy. I mean, I liked her because she was so fun, but I thought, the day that I get into trouble for being her friend is not going to be a happy day.


Pebulla and I spent the entire weekend together. She is okay, but so uptight. Everything for her involves thinking. When we heard the tune to "This Old Man" I got so excited, the way a three-year-old would. "Yeah! The ice cream truck is here. Let's go buy some ice cream!"

Pebulla sat quiet for much longer than I or the ice cream man could handle before saying, "Well, let's clean up the snakes and ladders board before we go."

I said, "You're kidding, right? The man will be gone by then. I have an idea, give me your money and I will go."

Pebulla started rummaging through her little mauve studded change purse. I didn't hear any coins, and it was much too small to hold any paper money. Then I heard "toot toot"—the departure warning from the ice cream man. I was more determined now than before to not have my only other friend come between me and my soft serve twist.

I pushed the game board over before stepping on it and running through the door. I heard Ms. Yearweb say something; I wasn't interested in hearing what it was. I kept running and running and running, not because I needed that ice cream, but because I felt like getting far away from Pebulla. If I didn't, I was sure I would regret what would happen next.

I didn't go back. I figured I'd see her on Monday. Between now and then I'd be able to come up with a believable story about why I didn't go back to her house on Saturday, and I might even have it in me at that point to apologize. I certainly couldn't find an apology right then as I saw the ice cream truck turn onto the main street en route to a place that I didn't have the energy to run to.

On Monday I saw Leon at school. He was so big and so very nice too. I didn't talk to him much, only when I wanted to find out about Luanne. I asked him for his sister and he told me to call her. I couldn't right then. So I said that to him, but he walked away before answering me. He wasn't hanging with the boys and girls like he usually did while everyone else was in class. I went to class after making a mental note to call Luanne once I got home.

My last class was my worst subject, Latin. The only good thing about the class was all the fun I had. I would do everything in that class, except work, of course. At the end of that class, Pebulla and I skipped homeroom, where we had to return to for the last ten minutes of the day. We decided to start walking home instead.

There was a limo outside; it had stopped right in front of the school. I thought, how nice some idiot wants to get noticed. Why ride in a limo to a Junior High School? I couldn't see who was in it, and I would not even give the person the satisfaction of seeing me looking because, I believed, that was why they were leaving school in a limo.

Pebulla lived at 1996 Kleeshing Avenue and I lived at 1989. We lived within walking distance of each other but couldn't see each other's house. While we were walking we spotted a limo. It was the same colour as the one at school, but I couldn't be sure it was the same one. Pebulla went inside and I continued to walk. The limo was going north while I walked south. It slowed down, but the tint was so dark that I wasn't able to see inside.

Once in my house, I was exhausted from doing nothing more than going to school and coming home. Pebulla called me as soon as I took my jacket off.

"Have you talked to Luanne today?" she asked.

"No," I said.

Then Pebulla's mom picked the phone up and demanded that she come downstairs.

Pebulla said, "You heard that," and hung the phone up.

Pebulla lived with her mom. She was an only child. She never spoke of any family members, just her mom. Their house was three rooms big plus a bathroom—very small and very comfortable looking. Pebulla did everything inside, she hardly came outside, not even to play in her front yard. Her mom worked from home, she said, so we would hardly see her. It was good for Pebulla because she always had her mom around. I asked her where her dad was and she said she would rather not talk about it. She wasn't rude at all. She just got straight to the point all the time. I remember asking her why she didn't hang out with Luanne and me.

She said, "Luanne has problems, and I don't want them."

"What do you mean?" I asked.

"If you can't see them, I won't point them out."

I just left it that way. I really didn't care what she thought about Luanne because one thing was for sure, I liked Luanne and I thought she was a great person, with faults, just like everyone else, including me.

My mom and dad were making dinner when I got home. Well, mom was making dinner while dad sat at the table telling one of his many stories. His stories always happened when we were not around. This time he was telling mom about the boy with the large head whose parents hid him in the closet when guests came over, but this one time he came out because he was hungry, and all the guests jumped up and ran. The settings of dad's stories were actual locations, but the events were so out in left field that I laughed, but always wondered whether they were true. Dad was a really humorous guy, so the way that he told his jokes and stories definitely helped.

When I got to the kitchen, mom asked me why I was home so early. I reminded her that 3:30 p.m. was not early, before telling her that Luanne was not at school today and that's why I was able to come straight home with Pebulla. Mom asked why Luanne was not in school.

"Not sure," I said.

"Can you call to see if she is okay?"

"Sure, after dinner."

It was my turn to wash up, so I was able to buy some time before calling Luanne. I mean, I wanted to call her, but I really wasn't sure what to say: "Gee, thanks for getting me those flip-flops" or "How do you get stuff?" or "Are you a thief?" Really, what would I say?

I washed the dishes while sis cleared the table. It was Gregory's night to do nothing, and he did it so well. We all got along great. We had to because mom made it hard not to. If anyone of us did something wrong, we were all punished for it. If one of us wanted to go to a party or something, it was an all or none with mom. Since I didn't do parties, Greta and Gregory would go and I would hang out with Luanne or Pebulla until they were all partied out, then we would go home together.

After the cleaning was done, I ran upstairs; I had to share my room with Greta. Whenever she was done with her art, she would just walk into our room and crash on the bed. The room always seemed messy when she was in there. Just her presence made the place a mess. She hardly stayed upstairs, she was always in the basement doing the unknown and having us believe she was addicted to art.

"GREGA!" mom called.

"Yes?" I said.

"The phone is for you."

"Mom, I'm in the bathroom. Tell her to call back." I ran into the bathroom.

As I sat there, I realized that I could not keep avoiding Luanne and her problem. So I flushed the toilet and went downstairs.

Mom said, "It was Pebulla."

"Pebulla?!" I said." I waited for her to call back, but she never did.

I watched television and imagined being a model for a few hours before heading back upstairs. My room looked messy when I entered, so I knew Greta was close.

"How is Luanne?" she asked.

"I don't know! Everyone is asking me about Luanne, I'm not her keeper. Why doesn't someone call her?!"

"Geez, it was just a question, don't go off your rocker!"

I thought, maybe I should call Luanne, but that thought faded. I went to bed.

The next morning I awoke to a loud bang. Gregory thought it was kind to play 'The Grave Diggers' cassette at 7:30 a.m. It really wasn't! Since I wouldn't be able to sleep in all that noise, I went downstairs.

Mom, Dad, Greta and Leon were all down there.

"Where's Luanne?" I asked. No one answered. "Umm, excuse me people, where is Luanne?" Dad told me to keep my voice down, mom looked at me, and Leon completely ignored me. I sat down. No one was really talking, so I sat in silence as well.

Finally Leon said, "How could you?"

"How could I what?"

Leon went on to tell me that I was not a nice person.

"What? Me?" I said. "What are you talking about? Where is all this coming from?"

"Luanne's gone. She wants you to have all her stuff. WHERE IS SHE?"

"How the heck I am suppose to know?" I said.

"Well, she always said, 'When I go, I want Grega to have all my things.' "

"Why didn't you ask her where she was planning to go?"

"Because I didn't take her seriously."

"So how did I become a bad person in all this?" I asked. I sat quietly, trying to process the information and figure out how it became my fault.

Leon's voice erupted, "SHE MIGHT HAVE TOLD YOU, IF YOU WOULD HAVE BEEN A FRIEND AND CALLED HER, IDIOT!"

My thought process was interrupted by Leon's yell, but with it came the answer to my question.

Mom jumped in, "Well, arguing is not the answer right now, we need to find Luanne. We cannot assume that she ran away. We have to start talking to people."

I wished they weren't so concerned about her. What could she be thinking, leaving my family to worry? She has a brother, a mother and a father, and millions of family members all over the world. Let them worry about her. Luanne had made it into my bad books quickly. I mean reaaallly quickly. She probably wasn't getting enough attention from the stores, so she ran away. What is her problem? I thought.

Leon searched tirelessly for his little sister that day. He knocked on doors, put up flyers and called random numbers, but he was not any closer than he was in the morning.

I watched television. I should not have been so angry, but I was. Everyone was asking about her the day before, did anyone call after all the questioning? I'm sure they didn't. I wondered when she left. Why she didn't call me? Well, she might have, but I was at school, like most normal teenagers. Her parents weren't even trying to locate her, why are my parents helping? Damn it!

The day came to an end and Leon went home. I stayed awake for most of that night. I was not sure why, but by the time I went to bed, I was sure of one thing: I was really starting to miss Luanne. She could have at least said goodbye to me. It began to sink in; Luanne is gone.

In the morning, I immediately turned to my notepad, hoping that I would find answers from its blank pages. Instead, I came up with a rhyme that was a little late, but will forever be true:

*Forever my friend you will always be,*
*Through good times through bad times you've understood me.*
*All our little talks so many secrets we've shared,*
*No matter what happens I hope you'll be here.*
*The friendship we have is more than true,*
*Who could ask for more if she has a friend like you?*

I wasn't able to remind Luanne that she was the very best person that I had ever met, but the minute she comes back, that will be the first thing that I tell her.

It was going to be a week since Luanne and I last communicated, and we had no leads as to where she could have gone. Sally, Luanne's next-door neighbour, told us that she saw a grey limo circling the block on Friday. Someone else said that they saw a tall man with red hair leaving Luanne's house on Friday, just after 2 p.m. Pebulla's mom saw Luanne while we were at school, dressed in red, with a lot of makeup on. She had a Ghetto Blaster in her hand. When Pebulla's mom said hello to her, Luanne said nothing and crossed the street.

Luanne could have been anywhere. She had friends, but they were mostly school friends, and I knew of them. She had no problem meeting people, thanks to her looks and her personality, so she could survive out there in the big bad world. But I didn't want her to be out there. I wanted her to be in this neighbourhood, close to me.

I know when Luanne comes back. I will do everything differently. I will let her know that she doesn't have to get me anything. I will love her anyway. I'll let her know how beautiful she really is inside and out. For always choosing me first for her dodgeball team, for always trying to bring me into conversations, for inviting me to every party that she has ever been invited to, for making me feel prettier than I am, I will thank her for all that. I want to thank her now.

For the first time, I lost my strength; I cried for Luanne. I cried for her not being here for me, or being a phone call away, or being within my reach. I cried because I didn't know where she was, who she was with, why she walked away. I cried because Luanne might be in pain, I cried because I ignored her. Luanne might be silently planning her end too, and she might need me. I cried.

And for all those people who have plans to end it all, I cry.

# CoCooN
### By MedC Harry

When I was young, I always dreamed of becoming a Sanitary Engineer. I began to practice whenever I got the chance…and then reality came in the way of a dog. My dream of becoming a sanitation worker was marred, along with my skin, which was hanging from the mouth of my neighbour's English bulldog. It didn't take long before I realized my wound was not a random act received by an out-of-control dog. It was a specific command, given by an evil neighbour.

That summer was spent at my dad's place. Dad was the funniest. He would call us mid-morning to let us know that he would be coming to get us "jus' now." In dad's language, that meant any time between right now and midnight.

Dad did shift work. He would go into work before we roused and return during the game show Bumper Stumpers. We would be so excited when dad returned. Just having him there sleeping was the climax of our day. I would put barrettes in his hair and take pictures with him. When dad's nap was over, I couldn't resist; I told him that I gave him a beautiful hairstyle. Dad would forget my confession and we would go to Eaton's. He would be oblivious to his visible femininity. NS and I would not let him in on our knowledge of his outer appearance.

That summer consisted of nothing more than waking up, showering and watching game shows, but it was the best summer of my life. We went to one amusement park just before school began. We weren't ever thrilled to go because after the day ended, reality was about to return, HOME!

At home, disarray was the only positive. Mama would talk on the phone all the time, leaving us to worry about ourselves. When our dyspepsia set in and our stomachs' began to speak loud, mama would speak louder so she would not have to hear us or acknowledge our complaints. The minute I recognized my mother's home, I got an awry feeling, a feeling only a divine power could settle. I never really understood the feeling, then I met Maricu.

The day I met Maricu I was sitting in my room. Mama, to no surprise, was on the phone. Maricu brought me into another world. Together we became kids. We ate whatever we wanted to eat. There was no one around to speak louder than us, drowning the sounds of our innocent voices. We gained weight and felt good about every forbidden pound. I was allowed to smile, laugh, cry and love, all in the same hour when Maricu was around. Maricu always had time for GC. Maricu named me GC, "I am going to call you GC because you are." That was all that was said. No explanation offered, none initiated. It didn't matter what the letters stood for, I had been welcomed into a world known to many only in dreams.

NS and Maricu never met. A pity it was because they could have learned a lot from one another. I met Maricu's family once. They were very nice people, with many similarities to my family— same genders, similar sizes and ages. Maricu and I never once spoke about age.

Every time mama went on the phone her conversations would contain a whisper. With each whisper Maricu and I would tiptoe to the bottom of the squeaky stairs to hear which child was her target that day.

My other siblings tried to be perfect, attempting to keep their names out of mama's telephone conversations, but it never worked. It made things worse. Mama used it as an opportunity. She always wanted us to go astray, just to fit in with her friends. I would sometimes hear mama say things about one of her children; I could never guess who she was talking about because it was not a characteristic any one of us possessed. Maricu made me realize that the fables my mother created were similar to the life mama left behind.

I used to shed tears over mama's conversations, until Maricu and I met. One day when boredom overcame us, Maricu asked me if we could meet at the Wild Berry Tree. I wasn't sure how I would get there because, as much as mama stayed on the phone upstairs in her room, she always knew if we were in the house or not. I knew I would get there somehow though. So I opened the sliding back door and played very loudly before bringing the radio outside. After ten minutes of that, I left the music playing and ran out the big brown gate that served as my barricade to the outside world. That gate only served its purpose until I was eleven, then it started shrinking. It really was not that big.

Maricu and I got to the tree at the same time, I think. Although Maricu was of average size, being hidden by the full tree stump and wearing camouflage clothing might have been the reason her shadow did not show.

At the tree we came upon a large spider web. In my innocence, I began to examine the web. It was covered with debris from the tree and impossible to see through. I asked Maricu if spider webs could ever be that thick. Maricu began to explain the chrysalis stage, in a language that any mammal would understand. We used a magnifying glass to see the inside of the insects' home.

"One day these long wormy things will leave the nest and fly away, never to return to captivity again."

"They don't look like they could fly very far."

"GC, this just proves looks can be wrong."

I became very interested in the story of worms without wings flying away. We made the Wild Berry Tree our meeting place. I began going there even without Maricu. Each time I arrived, Maricu would appear shortly after. I was usually armed with my own magnifying glass. Whenever I had my magnifying glass, Maricu did not have one. We never looked at the chrysalis sheath together. We would take turns, using one glass, looking for different details.

Maricu would never see what I saw, and I could never find what Maricu saw. Each time I went to the Wild Berry Tree, the worms were there. I was anticipating the growth of their wings. I did not think it was possible, but Maricu was so convincing, I just had to believe.

I used to quiver when I thought about the mental and emotional strain I would face once I left the Wild Berry Tree. But Maricu never failed to temporarily minimize the feeling.

One evening when I got home, I entered just in time to be accused of stealing fizz pops from Plackie's Convenience Store. I knew the truth, Maricu knew the truth, but mama believed what her imagination told her. I escaped to the room I shared with NS. Mama came too. She came with an extension cord. My skin had lacerations for at least two days, but that never stopped me from going to the Wild Berry Tree. Each day I went, I would return to a house of arraignment. Wounds would cover my skin each night and I would find comfort with Maricu each Wild Berry Tree day.

Summer arrived, the best season of my year. We returned to dad's house, but this summer was different. We were sent back each day, and returned only when dad was in our area. We were told it was because we were getting older, but NS failed to believe that. "Dad does not like us anymore." I believed. So now I was convinced that living was a punishment, wounds were received involuntarily and parents stopped loving their children.

We tried to make the best of it because when dad was around, no one alive or dead could make us believe that we were not the most blessed children on the earth, and dad supported our conviction.

When NS, dad and I went out, we used to visit dad's friends. They always made the most of us. We were given dinner, lunch, breakfast—in any order—something unheard of at home. When we went out, if we got too hot, dad would hold our jackets. Simple, but unheard of when mama was around. Dad would buy us snowflakes and snacks, depending on how long we were out. If we said we were hungry, he would give us options. Sometimes that meant home-cooked food. But the luxury of having options was so foreign we accepted the home-heated meals.

It was the week after school ended for the summer break. Dad had to work the afternoon shift, but since he was in the area he stopped by mama's place to see us. When we went outside to hug and kiss and make the most of dad, mama locked the door, which would leave dad with no choice but to take us with him. Mama knew dad would not leave us outside with the wild goats. Of course, NS and I would not have minded playing outside with the other kids in the neighbourhood, but dad would not allow that. He hated to see "the wild goats playing outside," as he would call them.

So Dad drove us to his friend's place. LW lived about a half an hour's walk from mama. Dad just dropped us off, told LW that he would be back after work, then left.

Like clockwork, dad arrived to get us around 11:30 p.m. He brought us to his house and we stayed there for the night. He dropped us off at mama's place around 2 p.m. Mama forgot to lock the door, so we walked in. She was not a happy dweller at that point, but that's okay. I was happy because I would get to see my source of sanity: Maricu!

Maricu and I went to check on the worms that fly. Not much had changed, only that there seemed to be more this time. Other folks began to come over to our spot to see what the fascination was all about. Some knew the story of the worms; others were too focused on the opposite sex to care about thick white webs in trees. It was good that way because I had Maricu's company all to myself.

Maricu and I walked around the neighbourhood before going home. Down by the second parking lot we discovered crystals beside an old car. It was the coolest thing ever. I started gathering them from the passenger side while Maricu examined the ones on the driver's side. During my gathering I cut my finger. Just then Maricu came to my side to let me know that our discovery was not as profound as I had thought. The crystals were actually shattered glass from the car right beside us with the two broken windows. It all made sense. I had to go home to get my finger looked after. I was not quite sure how I was gonna clean it without mama wondering what I was doing. I tried anyway.

I got some toilet paper to catch the red drip before I started rummaging through the closet. I found this green ointment, not sure of the name. Poured some on my finger and nothing happened. So I put it back and went for the brown stuff, Dettol. Nothing happened. I was hoping for the same sensation I would get when mama would clean my open sores. You know, a burning sensation that was felt way down in the toes and then way up in the head. After pulling out the ammonia, the clear liquid way in the back of the closet, I got that sensation. Boy did I get it, so much so that mama hung the phone up after my yelp and came running out of her bedroom. I tried to wish the water in my eyes away, but the water had nowhere to go but on my shirt.

Mama asked me what happened. I told her, and then the belt came out. Yes, I know, I should not have been outside in the first place. Mama thought it was necessary to remind me with each whip of the belt, but I thought I had already paid for it by getting a crystal cut. Mama didn't think so.

The next day was Sunday. Maricu came to the window to find out if I was coming out. I thought I was, but mama had better plans for me.

Sundays meant a 9 a.m. wake-up via the Electrolux vacuum cleaner. Mama never cleaned on any other day of the week except Sunday mornings when 9 a.m. came, before we were awake.

If we were already up ironing our church clothes and preparing for our shower, mama would be in bed. If we were not awake yet and seemed like we would skip church, mama was and in the mood to vacuum, but only the upstairs hallway where our room was.

When the vacuum was not doing a satisfactory alarm clock job, mama would push our bedroom door open and say, "NO CHURCH TODAY!" Even if sleep was once there, it ran away with the thunderous no-nonsense tone of mama's voice. So off to church we went.

On Sundays the TV stayed off until at least 6 p.m., the time of the evening news. If mama went upstairs to carry on her phone monologue, I would turn it on just to see a face other than my own. I was in search of a face with colour so that I could feel more comfortable in my own living room. If mama was in a happy mood and she realized that the television was on, she would yell, "Turn it to Channel Two." Then she would come downstairs to make sure it was on TVO. That is when suffering really began. I blame my extreme cynicism and constant complaining on the reality that between the ages of eight to twelve I was sitting around watching whales swim and learning how deep the ocean could be. In my twenty-two years of life never once has anyone asked me to recall that information. It was well worth it!

As of Monday, it was back to book searching, looking out the window—with permission—and making garbage.

By the time the Back to School flyers were delivered, I was more than ready to return to school. My summer had come to an end over thirty times (every day of the month). Dad had stayed away for about three weeks. He called on the weekend to tell us that he was coming "jus now."

Mama gave us specific instructions: if LW is in the car, run back inside and lock the door. About two hours after dad called, NS and I went to take out legitimate garbage. On our way to the big green bins, we saw dad's little gold sports car coming down the street, and there was another head in it. NS and I looked at each other, dropped the garbage and ran back home. Once in, we locked the door. Dad hardly ever knocked on the door. He really didn't have too; when we heard his muffler, we were out on the curb awaiting his drive up the shared driveway. This time was different. Dad knocked, and when no one answered, dad knocked some more, When we moved the front curtain, dad waved and he kept knocking. Dad's fuse was very short, so for him to triple package his knocks, that was huge.

Dad continued to knock for a while after that, and when I heard his engine rev up I knew it…Dad was gone, for good. Again, mama struck again! That summer was so rocky that I wished school was around all year. Dad left an answering machine message to let us know that his company picnic was that day. Very disappointed was my response.

One PD day, dad came to get us, as he so faithfully did. Don't get me wrong, he was never on time, always late, always in a hurry to leave, always on his way to nowhere, but he always arrived at some point. That day was no different. He came to get us around 9 p.m., although we began our "daddy routines" around 2 p.m. As we were walking out the door, mama said, "Don't come back!" Dad never paid her any mind; actually, I think it would be fair to say dad had become so use to ignoring her that he was deaf to the sound of her voice. Anyway, dad's rush was warranted this time. He had to work the overnight shift, which meant he had to be on the freeway going towards the next borough by nine.

The way dad dealt with his difficulties, which appeared to be few, was to have a silent plan of action. He took us north, and in five minutes we had arrived.

He left us with LW and promised to return after work. I fell asleep right away because that's just what I do. Around two a.m. I was awakened. NS said, "get up, we gotta go." Being the clueless child that I was, I got up to go. Where I was off to was still unknown.

When I got downstairs, dad's friend was crying. There were two teenagers in the house; one was a mess and visibly angry, and the other was nowhere to be found. After standing there for a while, I finally woke up. NS was frightened while telling me that dad's friend was going to jail. I told myself that one of the two teenagers was the reason for the overnight melee, but I soon clued into how wrong I really was.

Mama had struck again. She'd found out that we were there and called the cops. She told them that we had been kidnapped or something like that. LW's youngest child was not MIA, but BWI, being wrongfully interrogated because of NS and me. The eldest child was up next.

We later found out that mama voiced many concerns, one being that she was afraid that we would be touched. After all the

51

statements were completed, we were taken to the phone booth at the corner where mama was standing, all decked out in her house robe and a pair of stockings on her head.

As NS, mama and I stood waiting for the outcome, dad hysterically arrived. Completing only three and a half hours of a ten-hour shift did not allow him to use any smile muscles. Dad was furious. NS was observing and, as always, I was clueless and in need of sleep.

Dad's friend was so hurt. We did not get to visit for a long time after that. Every summer, life would take another drastic turn, usually for the worse. That Friday night ended our weekend. Inside, we would sit around looking for things to do, people to play with, rooms to clean, and a book to read…well, maybe not the latter. Because I was the child who found pleasure in paper, I was occupied for about eight hours making paper people, booklets and little animals. Now I know this is called origami.

That weekend we really anticipated the arrival of school. NS and I had to create garbage when we wanted to go outside. We just collected items, threw them in a bag and called it garbage. Then walked to the green bins to dispose of the bag and stayed outside to play.

In the week that followed, there was not enough garbage to gather for us both to go outside. We had to make a tag team effort, but since NS was the most sought-after person in our "dimension" (that's what we called our little area of the complex), she would stay out for hours before she would give me some garbage. Sometimes, after hours complaining of boredom, mama would tell me to go outside, usually when a forbidden phone conversation was about to start. It usually included talk about dad or one of us, but that didn't matter, it got me outside with the big and small kids.

That is when childhood began. Our close-knit outdoor family brought me alive. We jumped rope, played stinger and chook. The former is the old name for slingshot. The latter is a game and name that we made up but didn't market. While we were outside, it was like heaven.

When NS and myself were plagued by internal drought and the main water was not on, which meant we couldn't drink from our garden hose, I would be the one to go inside to get enough water to dampen both of our throats. Sometimes I would not be allowed to go back out, other times I was. The rest of the day would be spent outside with NS and the gang. When everyone went inside after 10 p.m. and there was nothing else for us to do, NS and I went inside.

Turmoil met us at the door. Mama was still on the phone with the same person. A stench started to make its way through the house, and mama was oblivious, or shall I say immune, to the change in her environment. To mention it to mama would have been the same as talking to myself. It seemed as if everything I said fell on deaf ears. Even to talk to NS was like whispering to a large group and hoping that just one person would hear what I said and attempt to interpret what I meant, all without every saying a word.

I began to search for something that I would enjoy doing. (I am still searching!) But that was the year I found out a lot about myself, mainly what I didn't enjoy doing: baking, sewing, reading, playing and being. I did enjoy writing though:

### THE WORLD

*This world is flat and bright*
*People shine in every light*

*No one had a zest for living*
*Chances are not given*

*Smiles are received every day*
*Strangers know what to say*

*Sincerity is not hard to find*
*No word spoken is unkind*

*Everyone knows each other's name*

*No one receives any fame*

*Competition does not exist*
*Laughter tops every list*

*There is no such thing as sin*
*Happiness is found within*

*Money has no value*
*Everyone finds something positive to do*

*Sickness is just a word*
*Yelling cannot be heard*

*Death is an extension of life;*
*Maximum gain and minimum strife*

*Equality is shared by all*
*No one can ever fall*

*Guns have not been made*
*Memories do not fade*

*Superiority is only a dream*
*Violence has not been seen*

*Darkness never appears*
*No one has any fears*

*Friends are not mandatory*
*Everyone gives praise and glory*

*Sundays' are twice per week*
*Evil we do not seek*

*The future is not guaranteed*
*Everyone knows how to read*

*Tears need not be shed*
*Insults are left unsaid*

*Anger is not expressed*
*Everyone does his best*

*Stress can be relieved*
*Gifts are not received*

*This world in which I speak is held quite dear*
*This world in which I speak can never disappear*
*This world in which I speak I will never stray*
*This world in which I speak I occupy every day*
*This world in which I speak is Mental, needless to say.*

❧

The worms were taking such a long time to disappear. I was getting really impatient.

"There time has not come yet. One day you will come here and see that they are gone. They are still in the early stages of their life. Give them time."

That was Thursday. So I did.

I returned on Saturday morning, Maricu was already there. We had a long conversation, and not once did we examine the worms. Maricu told me the world needed to be explored and now was the best time for it to be done.

"You will be fine! But always remember, *My angel rarely included coming up.*" I was given a hug for the first time. Then Maricu disappeared before I was able to lament. That night my eyes were heavy, not with sleep but from stale tears and swelling. I didn't know if Maricu would return. I didn't get a chance to ask what GC stood for, the angel quote was not explained, and I felt like Maricu was gone for good.

The next day I went back to the Wild Berry Tree. I made myself believe that Maricu would show up; it always happened that way. I waited in vain. Maricu never showed up. To my surprise, the worms were gone, and so was the chrysalis sheath. I went home after hours, and mama didn't say anything. The feeling was so strange I went back out, but this time I passed the tree and went to Maricu's house. It looked different. The lady who answered the door looked nothing like any of the people Maricu introduced me to. In fact, this person said she has never heard of Maricu. I was confused. This lady made it seem like I had escaped. I pleaded with her to tell me where Maricu was. She closed her door as calmly as she had opened it.

Now, whenever I need company, I always invite Maricu.

As the years progressed, Dad became scarce, but we never stopped calling. That summer I got caught up with the world outside my house. The good part about living in geared- to-income housing was that no matter how late, how early, how cold, how hot, how wet or how dry it was outside, there was one guarantee: there would be at least one other outside, either a child or a person, who didn't realize their childhood was over. I spent my days outside, from morning until night.

Mama did not notice, or care.

# Drugs of Revenge
*By Tanya Browne*

It was raining in the night when I was in bed, trying to get some sleep. I could hear the wet balls of misery pounding on my bedroom window like they were trying to get in. I had come home from work late that night and couldn't wait to get in my warm bed. For some reason I couldn't fall asleep, even though I was very tired due to the long day. I guess I knew something was going to be wrong. Just as my heavy eyelids were about to drop, the phone rang. I waited for the answering machine to take the call: "Hi, I'm not home to take your call right now, but if you leave your name and number, I will get right back to you."

"Hi, doc, it's Maida. We have just…"

I didn't wait any longer for the machine to take the message. I immediately tore the covers off and picked up the phone. "Maida? It's me, what's wrong?"

"We have just found another body. It's another male in his early twenties…looks like another suicide."

"Where was he found?"

"In the broken-down warehouse on Gore Road. We need you to come right away."

"Okay, I'm going to be on my way shortly."

I hung up the phone and ran to my closet to get something to throw on. I rushed down the stairs, ran to my office near the living room and picked up my old medical bag that I'd had ever since I graduated from medical school. I then put on my coat and shoes and grabbed my umbrella. I got into my old beaten-up station wagon and headed to the scene of the crime.

Gore Road was dark, long and narrow. It was raining heavily, and that didn't make it easy for me to see when to turn or steer straight. The wipers ran across the windshield swiftly, and since the rain was so strong, the wipers weren't doing any justice. The rain was beating the windshield wipers in the constant battle. As I turned on the winding road, the bright flashing red and blue lights of the police cars dominated it. When I turned into the warehouse, I parked beside one of the police cars and ran out of my car.

"Dr. Kay Scarpetta," I said to a police officer as I held up my identification. "Where's the body?" I asked him. He pointed towards the entrance of the warehouse and I ran to it immediately. Maida was standing right beside the body when I went in and he filled me in on every detail.

"His name is Jessie Slader. We found his ID in a bag that was sitting on the floor. It had a jogging suit in it that had dope in one of the pockets."

"Has his family been notified yet?"

"Yeah, but they don't seem to care. They apparently disowned him a while back because of his drug habit. I remember I busted him once for selling drugs. He always seemed to be getting into trouble with the law…heck, if I was his parents, I would have disowned him too."

"How was he found?"

"Two teens were supposedly coming in here to hang out and saw the body sitting up against a box. They got scared and called the police immediately."

"What were they doing out here so late at night anyway? I said in a suspicious tone, as if I was accusing them of something.

"I don't know." Maida looked at me and shrugged his shoulder. "Who knows why teens do the things they do today."

"Where are they?"

"They're outside. The police are questioning them right now."

"Do you think they know him or were with him when he died?"

"No. My guess is that if they did, they wouldn't have stuck around or even called the police."

I then turned my head and looked at the body. "So they think it's another suicide, hah?"

"Yep, that's what it looks like."

I reached into my medical bag and pulled out my gloves. When I put them on, I kneeled close to the body and started my examination. "Doesn't have any trauma to the head or any fractures on his arms or legs, except for a bruise on his left arm, which appears to be caused by the needle." He appeared to be in his early twenties and was wearing a black T-shirt with a picture of Charles Manson on it. His jeans were torn at the knees and smelled like Eternity, the men's cologne. He was propped up against a crate and had a needle lying right beside his left arm. He looked relaxed and probably died instantly after the heroine entered his body. "I guess I would say this is another drug overdose."

"Yeah, I guess so." Maida said, as he rolled his eyes in the back of his head. I could tell that Maida was fed up with these types of cases. Jessie Slader had been the third body we had found in the last month. The first guy was Melvin Taylor, who was also found in a warehouse and died from a drug overdose. The second guy's name was Eddie Matthews, and he too died from a drug overdose. Maida was a tall, medium-built man with brown hair and hazel eyes. His first name was River; he told me that his mother named him that because she liked the way rivers flowed, so calm and peacefully. Ever since his mother died, he preferred to be called by his last name because River brought back too many memories.

"What's wrong with these guys in their twenties?" I said with disgust.

"I really don't know, doc, I really don't know."

After I examined the body, I immediately went home. When I got there, I could see that the lights in my house were on. "I know I didn't leave them on," I said with uncertainty in my voice. I slowly walked up to the door and quietly turned the key. As I entered, I picked up a statue from the table in the hall. I was ready to use it on whomever was in my house. I slowly turned to my right and entered the dining room. There was no one there. I left the dining room and walked down the hallway and into the living room, where I saw that the television was on. Right when I was turning around to go to the kitchen to grab a knife, I screamed.

"Hi, Aunt Kay."

"What…what are you doing here?" I said, as I held my chest and took a deep breath. "Do you know that I could have hit you with this thing?" I held up the statue for her to see, and then I put it down.

"I'm sorry, Aunt Kay, I didn't mean to scare you. But remember I told you I was coming for a visit."

"Oh! I forgot." I could feel my forty-five-year-old face turning red. "I'm sorry, Lucy."

Lucy was my niece; she lived in Miami and tried to visit me whenever she had the chance. She was now eighteen; the last time I saw her she was just fifteen. She didn't have her thick glasses anymore, only contacts. I was pleased by the fact that she was starting to look more like a woman than a tomboy. The one thing that I noticed the most was that she coloured her beautiful dark brown hair, blond.

"Lucy, your hair looks lovely," I said as I brushed my fingers through it. I really didn't like it, but I just acted like I did because I didn't want an argument.

"Do you really think so, Aunt Kay? It's the same as yours. Now it will look like you're my mom," she said as she rapped her big arms around me and gave me a hug.

I really didn't know what to say, so I just hugged her back. Lucy's mother was my younger sister Dorothy. Dorothy always put her relationships first, and Lucy was always last choice. Her mother always made her feel like she wasn't loved and Lucy hated her for that. Even though I lived in Virginia and she lived in Miami, I acted more like a mother to Lucy, but I didn't want her to call me that.

"Oh Aunt Kay, there's someone I want you to meet. Her name is Paulina Jenkins. She's a friend of mine." I was shocked because Lucy never had friends before. She was a tomboy whose friend was her computer.

Her friend came out of the living room. "Hi, Miss Scarpetta."

"Hi, Paulina," I said, with my eyes wide open and my hand stretched out for her to shake it. Paulina was a tall, skinny girl who had unusually big brown eyes, with a small narrow nose and a little mouth. Her eyebrows were thick and dark, and her eyelashes were long and straight. They almost looked like the fake ones they sell in the stores. Her hair draped over the side of her face and she had a crooked smile. She shook my hand, and Lucy said they were going to spend the night and go to Paulina's house later on in the day.

"So, Paulina," I said, "what brings you here to Virginia?"

"I decided that I want to live with my mother and maybe finish school here. There are also some old friends I would like to see." I smiled at her, and she returned it with her crooked one. I stayed up to talk to them a while longer and then went off to bed because I was tired. When I hit my pillow, I instantly fell asleep.

I only got three hours of sleep, and all I could think of was getting home early to get to bed. I got to work around 7:30 a.m., and as I entered the hallway of the morgue, I could tell that I was the only person there. No one was there to greet me with the usual cheery good mornings; there were only the bright fluorescent lights of the hallway shining down on me. As I walked further into the hallway, I passed the stainless steel refrigerator and opened the door to the autopsy room. I took off my coat and hung it up in my office. When I came out and turned to my left, I saw a gurney with a body in it, covered by a white sheet. I looked at the toe tag and saw Jessie Slader's name on it. I put on a pair of gloves and rapped my plastic apron around my waist.

Just as I was about to roll the gurney towards the machine to weigh the body, my assistant Debbie Bailey came in and greeted me the way she usually did. "Good morning, Kay. How are you today?" she said with a big smile on her face.

"Oh…I have had better days. I'm just so tired."

"So I guess we have just one case so far?"

"Yeah."

"Thank God," she said as she sighed in relief.

She walked over to the shelf and got her gloves and apron. She helped me weigh and measure his body, and after we wheeled it to the x-ray room across the hall. We transferred the body from the gurney to the table and pulled off the sheet. The body was starting to stink. I started to examine his head first and worked my way down. I noticed that he had a bump on his left middle finger, which indicated that he wrote with his left hand. The bones in his right hand had been broken. I could tell by the way they looked that they were beginning to heal, but he didn't have a cast. I then saw the needle mark, the size of a pinhole, on his left arm. I thought that was strange.

After we did the rest of the autopsy, Debbie left and I cleaned up. I started to think about the case. "How could he be left-handed and have the needle mark in his left arm?" I said to myself, puzzled. "Especially if his right hand was broken and he couldn't use it." When I was finished cleaning up, I went into my office and called Detective Maida. The phone kept ringing, and as I was about to give up there was an answer.

"Detective Maida speaking."

"Hi, Maida, it's me, Kay!"

"Hi, Doc, did you get to examine the body?"

"Yes, I did, and I have to talk to you about something. Can we meet at my house after I come home from work?" I whispered into the phone.

"Yeah sure, doc," he said.

"Okay, I'll see you then, bye."

After work I went straight home. Lucy was there so it gave us more time to talk. "So where did you meet Paulina?" I said, just to start a conversation.

"I met her at school. She took some computer classes with me, and we just started talking and hanging out. Then we became friends. It's nice that she wants to live with her mother. Isn't it, Aunt Kay?"

"It is nice, but is she the only child?"

"Now she is. Her brother was killed here a couple of years ago. She took it really hard, and then moved to Miami."

"Oh, that's terrible. How did he die?"

"I don't know. She never really talks about it." She immediately changed the subject and started talking about something totally different. "So I was thinking, Aunt Kay, maybe I could come here and live with you."

Once again Lucy caught me off guard. I didn't know what to say. "Well...I...I don't think you can!" I said fumbling with my words.

"Oh, come on, Aunt Kay. It would be fun," she said with a big smile on her face.

I got up from the table and walked to the kitchen to start dinner, "No...I don't think it's a good idea." I could see from the corner of my eye that Lucy's smile turned into a frown. She got up from the chair and charged towards me, like she was a bull chasing a red flag.

"So you're rejecting me too, just like my mother always does?" she yelled as she looked at me wildly, her blue eyes filling up with tears.

"No, Lucy, I am just saying it's not a good idea," I said as I started to move towards her to comfort her.

"Just when I'm finally happy in my life, you want to ruin it." She immediately turned around and stormed off to the door. "I'm going out, don't expect me back any time soon!" she said, as she slammed the door behind her.

"Lucy! Come back," I yelled out loud. "I guess I'll just give her time to cool down," I said as I furiously chopped up the onions.

I cooked dinner and set the table for Maida and me. I then took a shower, and when I came out, the doorbell rang. I slipped on my night robe and went to the door. I peeked out the peephole and saw Maida's thirty-five-year-old face staring into it. I opened the door and greeted him. "Thanks for coming."

He looked at me curiously with his hazel eyes and said, "What's wrong, doc? Are you okay?"

"I'm a little tired, but I'm fine."

"Well, when you called me, I thought something was really wrong."

"Something kind of is. Oh, don't just stand at the door, come in, come in. Sit down and relax. I cooked dinner for us. I'm just going to go upstairs to put on some clothes and I'll be right back to tell you what's going on."

When I got downstairs, Maida was pacing back and forth in the living room. I went into the kitchen and took out some food. I placed it on the table and sat down.

"Well, doc, aren't you going to tell me what the hell is going on?"

"Of course, have a seat." I said as I motioned my hand towards the chair. "It's about the Slader case. I don't think he was alone when he took the drugs. Actually, I think he was murdered." I looked at him sternly, waiting for him to respond. "Remember the needle hole I showed you in his arm when we were at the warehouse?" Maida nodded as he waited for me to explain myself. "Well, it turns out that Jessie was left-handed and there is no way he could have put the needle in with his left hand. The other thing is his right hand had been broken, and in order to use the drugs, he needed help to do it."

"So either he was murdered or a person who helped him fled after they saw he was dying. Either way, it's still a crime," he said. "Hey doc, do you think the other cases are linked to this one?" he said as he widened his eyes at me.

"You mean the two suicide cases before this one?"

"Yeah. But then again, with Melvin Taylor and Eddie Matthews there were no suspicious circumstances," he said with a frown.

"Well I would say our killer got sloppy," I said with a smile.

"I guess so," he said as he picked up his fork and started to dig into the food. "Mmm…this is good," he said, smiling back.

We finished eating our dinner. Maida got his coat and shoes and was ready to leave. "I'll make sure I try to find a connection between Jessie and the other two cases so we can solve it, if it's murder. Thanks for dinner, I'll see you tomorrow. Oh doc, you got a light?"

"You know I quit smoking a couple of years ago, and I thought you did too." I reached over and pulled the cigarette out of his mouth.

"I did, but I have to stay alert for this case. We have a murder to solve." He grabbed the cigarette out of my hand and walked through the door.

I always knew Maida to be that way. Whenever he had a big case to work on, he smoked non-stop and became a workaholic. As soon as he left, I locked the door and miserably waited for Lucy to come home. I hated being alone. I have been alone for almost all my life. My first marriage failed miserably, and any relationship I have turns out to be a disaster. And when everything's going fine, something happens to screw it up.

Lucy came home fairly late that night, and it wasn't until the afternoon when I received a call about my next case. Maida called and told me that there was a body found on May Street. He said it was outside a factory that made plastic supplies. The victim's name was Jeffery Parker, a twenty-one-year-old college student. He was found propped up against the side wall of the factory facing the train tracks. There was a needle found at the left side of his body. He apparently went missing from home two days ago and his mother called the police. A man who worked in the factory found his body and notified the police.

When I examined his body the day he was brought to the morgue, I noticed that he had a fibre caught in his nail. I put it in an evidence bag and waited for work to be finished so I could tell Maida. It was a little cotton fibre that must have come off the killer's clothing. The victim had a tiny scab on his left arm, and small bruises on the back of his neck and on his left arm. Someone grabbing and squeezing probably caused the bruises found at the back of his neck. I could see the pattern of fingerprints on it and I could tell it was the person's right hand because of the positioning of the marks. The bruises on his arms were caused two days ago, which was the day he went missing. From examining his body, there was no doubt in my mind that he had been murdered two days ago.

I called Maida and told him about the fibre that I found in the victim's nail and I told him that I thought he was murdered.

The night that I got home from work the phone rang. I rushed to the phone before the person could hang up.

"Hi, doc it's me," he said with excitement in his voice. "I think I finally found a connection between all the victims."

"Well, I'm listening." I said.

"Melvin Taylor, Eddie Matthews, Jessie Slader and the latest victim, Jeffery Parker, were all friends. I was looking through the police records to see if all of them have been arrested at least once, and they were. It appears that they were all arrested for the negligent homicide of Bruce Walker and then fleeing the scene. Apparently, this happened three years ago. Bruce Walker was just fourteen years old. They never made it to trial because all of a sudden the evidence went missing. Doc…doc…doc? Are you still there?"

"Yeah, Maida, I'm still listening." I was trying to remember the case and it slowly started coming back to me. "There was a fifth guy involved, wasn't there?"

"Yeah, doc, his name was Anthony Sanchez. But what does that have to do with anything? He's not dead."

"Maida, don't you get it? The killer is still after him. For whatever reason, they are trying to kill all the people that were involved in that case, unless there's some other connection."

"You know what, doc? I think you're right. I think we should keep a close eye on Anthony Sanchez before he gets bumped off too. I remember when the case was dismissed. The reporters interviewed the family of the victim. His sister, Paula Walker, took it hard and said that someday they would get theirs," he said with a giggle. "And they sure did."

"Well, what happened with her?"

"Her and her family left town. They couldn't handle living in that house anymore."

Anthony Sanchez was on Killington Avenue and Detective Maida and I followed him to keep a real close eye on him. Anthony entered one of the late-night clubs and stayed in there for quite a while. When he came out he was not alone. He was with someone dressed in a long black trench coat that was open in the front. They walked into an alley that was right beside a warehouse. Maida and I then rushed towards the alley but did not see them.

We were just about to turn around when we heard a loud scream. It was Anthony Sanchez. When we found the side entrance to the warehouse, we entered and saw Anthony lying down on the floor holding his arm. When I looked at his arm, I saw a needle sticking out of it. The person in the long coat was standing still, with their back towards us. Maida then told me to hide behind a crate, so I did.

"Put you hands up and turn around, nice and slow," Maida said as he pointed his gun firmly at the criminal.

The tall black figure started to turn slowly with its hands in the air, then it reached into its pocket and drew out a gun.

The next thing I heard was the sound of Maida's gun firing at the murderer. The body collapsed to the ground, and we both rushed to it.

When I saw who the person was, I was totally shocked. It was Paulina Jenkins, also known as Paula Walker. She was wearing a short black skirt with a low-cut top and an open sweater over it. I stayed there with my mouth open, looking at the dead body of what use to be Lucy's only friend.

Maida then dialed the police on his cell phone.

"What am I going to tell Lucy?" I said, tears flowing.

Maida turned to me and asked, "You know this person?"

"Yeah. She was Lucy's friend."

Paula Walker was brought to the morgue the next morning. I didn't work on the body because it didn't seem right. I was all shaken up. Lucy was devastated when I told her the news. She was leaving for Miami that afternoon.

I felt sorry for Paula because she had so much hate in her that all she wanted was revenge. She was the girl on the news saying that "they'll get theirs," and I guess she was right. She apparently blamed those guys for her brother's death because they supplied him with the drugs and then left him to die when they saw he was dying.

Anthony Sanchez survived but was in the hospital. Reporters were everywhere, trying to get the story, and I just decided to book my vacation time. I think I will go on a trip with Lucy to get her mind off all this, and I hope it happens soon.

# Introduction to the Edge
*By Michael W. Polack*

I was sitting in my office, thinking of nothing in particular. You know how it is when stuff floats around in your head. You think about your job, your house, your horse, your friends and your man, or your woman. I was lucky enough to have the middle three (not the man), struck out on the last, and not too sure about the first sometimes.

I'm a detective, you see. Oh, not one of your everyday garden-variety PIs, but a licensed MPI. That's magical private investigator, for those of you who are lost in time. Not that I'm the best one, mind you. I think I've concentrated on personal spells of offense and defense more than most, but in terms of raw power or ease of access to the void, maybe top third.

This puts me in a tough spot. The rich guys always hire the best, and I'm a little high-priced for the little guy. That just leaves the merchants for me and two hundred other MPIs to fight over. Oh well, it pays the bills.

So here I am, not expecting much and then *she* walks in and changes everything. Long and lean and mean. She moved with the controlled power that usually means enforcer, or even assassin. You just know that once the claws were unsheathed, the flesh would really fly around that one.

"What can I do for you?" I asked in a voice suddenly gone hoarse. The husky music that answered me matched the figure I was glimpsing through her long, black cloak—tight black jerkin fighting the pressure of firm, rounded globes of perfection.

"I said, I want to hire you." The sexy drawl brought me back from dreamtime.

"Huh," was my witty reply. "I mean, sure. What for?" I was willing to do anything but sell my soul for her. And I'd consider renting it to her for a while.

"Have you ever heard of Francis Ruttidge?"

"Sure, who hasn't," I replied. Francis only owned most of the world. And had the rest wrapped up, compounded and in his pocket.

"I want to kill him!"

If she'd dropped down and laid an egg, I couldn't have been more surprised. "I think you're in the wrong place, honey. I don't do hits."

She smirked, "I'll make the hit, I just need you to find him for me."

So, I guess I was right. She was an assassin with a capital A if she wanted Francis Ruttidge. I suddenly had a frightening thought—I'd seen her face. I knew who she was. If I said no, she certainly wouldn't want my ugly mug alive to identify her.

"What do you want to do that for?" I said, buying time. I started rubbing my fingers on my desk. After her eyes disregarded that motion, I started gathering energy from the void. Most people would see me making vaguely suggestive movements with my hands. Other practitioners would have seen me grapple with the furtive, slippery, coloured whorls that magic in its raw form looks like. A sort of aurora borealis. I have found that practice negates the need for all that spell mumbo-jumbo, for me anyway. Just concentrate and away you go. I must have made too obvious a movement because a short sword or a long knife grew out of her hand and stopped a mere inch from my throat.

"They call me Edge," she said, "and you won't need whatever it is you were going to do."

One thing about magic, it requires concentration. And when someone is fast enough to draw a weapon with a very sharp point and shove it in your face before you take a breath—well, your concentration just naturally deserts you.

I opened my hands in an appeasing (I hoped) way. "Just trying to save my secretary cleaning up my remains tomorrow morning."

"If I wanted you dead, you would be already."

Boy, did I believe her. She made the weapon disappear as fast and as mysteriously as she had made it appear.

"I told you, I need your help!"

I leaned back in my chair. The least I could do was hear her out.

"When I was little," she started out, "killing people was the furthest thing from my mind. I lived in the city of Minden. My father was a blacksmith, and a thriving one. As you know, life in the big city is no picnic, and everyone needs weapons, cutlery, iron bars, horseshoes, etc. Anyway, I first learned about weapons at my father's knee. How to make them. How to care for them, and how to respect them for what they are—instruments, but deadly instruments in the right hands.

Anyway, my dad wanted to expand. So he went to a banker. A very well-respected banker—Francis Ruttidge. He got his money and expanded his business. He began to rake in the money, and then, there were break-ins. Money was stolen on the way to the bank; customers were harassed. It was a systematic program aimed at my dad's business, and it worked. The bank foreclosed after debts started to pile up. They wouldn't lend him the money to pay for protection. As soon as the smithy belonged to Francis, the thievery stopped and the money rolled in again.

We found out later that Francis had engineered the whole thing. My dad went after Francis with an axe and was taken apart by that pack of wolves he calls business associates. That left me, and what was left of dad's property.

When Francis had himself made my guardian, everyone said what a saint he was to take me in after my dad had snapped and tried to kill him. I was about fifteen then, and starting to grow up and fill out. Francis was looking at me in a more than fatherly way. One night, he came to the house drunk. He came straight up to my bedroom and tried to rape me. I took his knife from his belt and tried to put it between his eyes. I got this instead."

I looked to her chest where she was pointing. I noticed for the first time that what I had taken for a necklace pendant was in fact a bronzed human ear.

"So you see," she said in a tightly controlled voice, "I owe him for my father's life, his business, my lost childhood, and everything that has come after."

"How did you come by your present, ah, skills?" I asked.

"When I ran away, leaving Francis bleeding like a stuck pig, I got lost in the warrens of an unfamiliar neighbourhood. Some street punks started chasing me. I ran and ran until I got backed into a dead-end alley. The five of them spread out in a semi-circle and started walking toward me. Suddenly, an old man in a black cloak materialized out of the darkness beside me. He made no sound, just stood there. The largest tough slid a sword from his sheath and the others followed suit. The old man stepped forward, and the circle closed around him. As the leader lunged at him, he melted to the side and a leg shot out. There was a sharp crack and one of the youths folded to the floor of the alleyway. As swords flashed in the lamplight, I could barely follow the old man's movements. His hands and feet were blurred weapons, breaking ribs and arms and legs. Twenty seconds after it had started, it was over. There was a pile of groaning garbage littering the ground and the old man was barely breathing hard. I wanted that power like I'd never wanted anything before. He took me in and trained me in his profession. His name was Hammermist."

For the second time that night my jaw dropped to my chest. That name was legend. The prices he commanded could buy small kingdoms. He had killed kings and queens. If you could afford his price, your enemy would die. If she had been trained by that, I'd better stay on her good side.

She coughed. Her gentle prod brought me back to reality.

"So where do I come in?" I asked.

"I've been following Francis' doings as I built my skills," she said. "I reached the point where I thought I could take him and his men about six months ago. But, he's disappeared. I need you to find him."

"Why me?" I said suspiciously.

"Well," she said with an engaging grin, "the ones who charge twice your price have almost certainly done business with Francis before or hope to do business with him in the future. Besides, you're honest—if you take a job, you'll do it."

Her line had a hint of flattery, but also a ring of truth. Before I knew what I was doing, I found myself agreeing.

৯০

I reached out for the void for the second time that night. This time, no shining implement of death appeared in her hands. I subconsciously relaxed and found the right focus. Shaping the energies I found there until they fit the spell, I threw it at the wall. It burst with a tangible, visible spectrum of colours and resolved into a translucent film of energy, about two feet by two feet. As I concentrated on a picture of Francis I'd built up in my mind, shapes began to swirl on the wall. With another flash of colour, the screen solidified into a picture of a large dining room. I saw Francis briefly before a backlash of energy stabbed at my mind. Quickly withdrawing before I was reduced to a babbling idiot, I caught a glimpse of the castle surrounding that dining room.

"What. What!" she exclaimed. "Didn't it work?"

"Please," I said, "my scrying spell is flashy but quite serviceable. No, the problem is— he's got magical protection." I kicked myself mentally. I should have expected it. "I did get a glimpse of that castle though. He's in the lands of Varg—about a fifty-mile journey from here through the roughest land you can think of. No wonder you haven't seen hide or heard from him for a while. Are you sure it's worth it to you?"

"It's worth it," she growled.

I had lived on the outskirts of Varg for much of my young life. I'd done everything I could to get away from that godforsaken land and here she was, raring to go trekking through who knows what.

"I hope you think so once we start," I said. "Here's what we'll need..."

⁊

Her expression of surprise was comical on one who deals in death. I guess I dress like a dandy to get as far from my countrified beginnings as possible. Of course, fancy clothes and wilderness hikes don't go together, but I guess she didn't expect it. I had on brown and green camouflage breeches made of the finest deer hide. They would keep me warm, allow me to blend in with the forest we would be in for the next few weeks and help to cover up my man smell. A matching brown shirt was covered with a warm bearskin vest. A bow was strapped across my back, along with a quiver of steel-tipped hunting arrows. A knife was on my right hip and a rapier on my left. A coil of rope was thrown over my left shoulder behind my pack. Supple but tough leather boots completed the look. She was wearing her outfit of the night before, with the addition of a long sword on her back. A pack complemented the sword.

I'd tied up my affairs in town for the next few months. My secretary was glad of the vacation, but not happy at being awakened at three in the morning to lend a helping hand. He was like that.

"Shall we?" I said, leading off to the north. "We'll hike for a couple of hours and then make camp. We'll need more than an hour of sleep where we're going. I feel funny calling you Edge," I said. "My name's Eliak, by the way. We had no time for formalities last night. Call me El, my friends all do."

"And you can call me Edge," she said, but I caught a slight smile on her face. This might not be the chore I thought it would be. Especially with the amount of money she was paying me. I'd be able to retire, or at least move to a better neighbourhood.

Edge was obviously fit, but hiking uses totally different muscles from the kind of exertions she was used to. I'd kept my fighting trim, so to speak, by periodic hunting trips. After our four hours of trudging through trees, we reached a clearing I vaguely remembered. Edge looked relieved when I threw my pack down and started gathering branches. I made a rude shelter against some dead brush and scattered some leaves over pine boughs for our bed.

"Where are you going to sleep?" she asked, eyeing the narrow confines of the shelter.

"In there," I replied.

"And where am I going to sleep?" she inquired with a quirk to her eyebrow.

"In there also," I said. "Look," I said quickly as her frown presaged some possibly nasty action with some weapon she had secreted on her person. "It gets cold out here and it's too dry for a fire. We wouldn't want to burn the forest down around us."

She looked at me kind of funny, but didn't say another word. I grinned from ear to ear. After she'd turned her back, of course.

I woke up to an increased difficulty in breathing and a mouthful of hair. "What's going on?" I said, spitting out the hair. "Get your elbow out of my stomach."

"What was that noise?" she said.

I could see the glint of moonlight on her naked blade. The eerie howling filled the night again. "It's just wolves," I said.

"Just wolves!" she screamed.

I'd forgotten she was a city girl. "Relax," I said, "they've got easier game than us." She lay down beside me again, much closer than before, but she kept the sword in her hand.

My second awakening was much more pleasant. Her head was nestled in my shoulder and her arm and leg draped over my body. I silently thanked the cold night and relaxed until she should wake up. I could get used to this.

The country we were passing through was beautiful but unforgiving. The nights were cold, even in midsummer. The only passage through the forest was by way of game trails. We could see the signs of life everywhere, but the animals were keeping out of sight.

We camped for our noon meal on the edge of a drop-off. A stream trickled suicidally over the edge to fall fifty feet to the vegetation below. As we ate journey cakes stuffed full of fruit, the silence around us entered our souls.

It seemed a crime to break it but I said, "What does it feel like?"

"What does what feel like?" Edge said with a guarded look.

"To kill someone," I said. I wasn't just prying, I was really curious.

"Haven't you killed anybody?" she countered.

"Yeah," I said, "but I mean for money."

"It's a job like any other," she said dryly. "I have hours where I work and hours to myself. I wish for better pay, better benefits, just like anyone else."

It was an evasion, but I let it be. "What will you do after you've killed him?" I said. Better to think positively from the outset.

"Settle down. Raise a family. Enjoy my money."

Edge's response indicated to me that she was younger than she seemed. Imagine, an idealistic assassin. "We'd better get going," I said, breaking the mood.

"You aren't going anywhere!" The voice coming from the trees at the edge of the clearing was low but more threatening for that very reason. A man stepped out of the trees, a loaded crossbow pointed in our direction. A second man stepped out some ten feet from the first. His crossbow was just as threatening.

"What do you want?" I said.

"It's not us," he said chuckling to his companion. "Kill them!" he growled, raising the bow.

Twin flames—flickering green—lanced from my hands and connected with the bows, incinerating them. It's not every magician who can aim raw chaos, I thought smugly. A slight breeze from beside me indicated that Edge wasn't asleep. A quivering handle had appeared in each man's eye. Left eye for the man on the right and right eye for the one on the left.

"Oh great," I said, "now we'll get some answers!"

Edge, ignoring me, retrieved her daggers and wiped them on the coarse jerkins of our would-be assailants. She then proceeded to check their garments and packs. I could hardly surpress a shudder. Man, was she cold.

Edge walked, or rather glided back to me—just like a damn cat. She showed me a sack of gold and a note. "It says 'Make sure they don't come back,' and it has a description of us," Edge said.

"Well, at least we know we won't be lonely," I quipped.

૭

I looked around for the flowers. Star-shaped and pink with white spots. Although it wasn't strictly necessary, the tea made from this particular flower would make it much easier for my mind to break the bond with my body and check out our surroundings.

"Ah, there they are," I said. Pulling a bunch, I put them in my makeshift pot, made from the bark of a nearby birch. The water in the bottom would prevent the fire from burning the wood. Now for the fire. A moment of concentration, a blue flicker on the canvas in my mind and a flame was flickering in the twigs beneath the pot. "Now remember, you have to protect my body. Normally, I don't do this out in the open," I cautioned. "See you when I see you."

I downed the brew in one gulp. Whew, it would never catch on in the bars. Then I closed my eyes and sat back against the bole of a tree. I could feel the peculiar tingling in my scalp. The drug affected every practitioner of the arts slightly differently, but that tingling was common to all. All I had talked to anyway. I felt my body relax, and I felt as if I were getting lighter. There was a feeling of stretching and then a light pop, as of suction being released. I was looking down at my body. Edge was touching my neck and looking concerned. A feeling of warmth suffused my non-body. It seemed that she was starting to have some feelings for me. What they were I could only hope to discover.

Taking one last look at the gentle rise and fall of my chest, I expanded my awareness. This is hard to describe to someone who's never done it. Imagine yourself as a balloon. Now imagine filling yourself with air to the bursting point. Now imagine yourself doubling that volume of air. Don't get me wrong, it isn't an unpleasant feeling—just intense. I drifted around the surrounding area, seeking out other life forms. This method of travel is much faster than any corporal method. A galloping horse would have had difficulty keeping up with me. Not to mention the effortless changes of direction and level. I found a small campfire about three miles south and west of our position. It was just a bunch of trappers.

As I circled back towards our camp, I found them. There were about ten of them. They were dressed much better than the last two. These looked like professional mercenaries who wouldn't be surprised like we'd surprised our deceased friends. They were wearing black boiled leather armor with metal plates riveted at strategic positions. While not offering as much protection as full mail, it would allow for more flexibility and comfort. I took in as many details as I could and prepared to move back to where Edge would be waiting, impatiently, I was sure.

A glimpse of a small fire in a sheltered corner of the encampment drew my eye. There, a man without any armor was just putting down a cup, a bunch of star-shaped flowers— pink with white spots—at his side. I hesitated. This camp was far enough behind us that we could lose them with a little luck and if we pushed on hard enough. But not if they had someone able to track our every move. And, if this magical practitioner was better than I, I'd like to find out sooner rather than later.

It is possible to affect the physical world from the spirit plane, but it is exceedingly difficult and burns a lot of energy. It was, however, much easier to affect another who was also in the plane. I moved swiftly to construct a cage out of the wisps of chaos that could be seen nearby. In this way, I would not only have something at hand to wield against my opponent, but I would denude the area of chaos, which he could use against me. I could see the dark outline as his spirit lifted from his body, and I was ready. I dropped the cage over the shadowy form and caused the bars to mesh seamlessly together. Well, dropped is the wrong word—willed is more like it.

As the other magician became conscious of the barrier surrounding him, I let myself be seen. Ouch, maybe that was a mistake. I physically (mentally?) felt him press angrily on my cage with his substance. A dull headache immediately started up in the back of my mind. This guy was strong. If I hadn't had the cage prepared, I don't think I could have held him. As it was, I was expending energy at a reckless rate. The way he was acting, it seemed like he had an infinite store. He suddenly changed tactics. An angry red probe—a narrow, focused beam of his thought— speared out at me. It was impossible to keep such a thing contained. It slid easily through my barrier and hurtled toward me. Without thinking, I knocked it aside. Looking down, there was a two metre sword of blue light in my right hand. I had wielded it effortlessly. I'd never done something quite like that before. I guess need really does breed invention. More of the red spears came my way. I knocked them aside just as easily.

Time for some action of my own. Gathering my energy, I willed the cage to contract. Black and yellow sparks flew when his substance met the confines of the cage. I "heard" his mental scream. In this form, the chaos that made up the walls of the cage were inimical to him. By contracting the cage, I was drawing off the energy he needed to subsist in this plane. In effect, I was killing him. I had realized that I couldn't let him go. It might seem cold, but he was stronger than me. If I let him go, I would be the one screaming in rage and frustration and, yes, pain. I did what I had to do. The cage constricted until, with a bright black flash, nothing was left inside. I barely saw the body by the fire tumble to the ground before I felt my own consciousness fleeing.

I woke up with a start. Edge was splashing cold water on my face. As the fuzzy edges of my thinking clarified, I realized that my spirit had snapped back to my body like an over-stretched elastic band. I felt like I'd run a marathon, and I had a whopping headache besides.

"What happened to you? One minute you're there, then you're gone for hours, then you're back and you keel over." Edge babbled on with a rising note of hysteria. I couldn't help myself, I laughed.

"What're you laughing at?" she snapped.

"I've never heard of a hysterical assassin," I replied, dissolving into half-hysterical laughter myself. The brush with death, even if it wasn't my own, had left me with a knowledge of my mortality. I knew, like I never had before, that I could die—no, *would* die someday. The laughter eased the absoluteness of that knowledge.

Edge stood abruptly and walked over to her pack. Grabbing her sword, she started towards the trees.

"Where are you going?" I asked, finally gaining control of myself.

"I didn't come here to be laughed at," she glared back at me.

"Wait!" I said. "I'm sorry." All I needed now was to lose whatever ground I had gained with her. I struggled to my feet and walked cautiously over to where she waited with a suspicious expression on her face. Closing my eyes, I concentrated. This was going to cost in my present state, but...fixing the image firmly in my mind, I coaxed the nearby strands of chaos into the form I wanted. This was different from my normal mode of operations.

This was much more precise, but just as difficult in its own way. "There," I said.

She took the rose from me with something like wonder in her face. It was perfectly formed. It had the colour and lustre of a bit of good metal heating in the forge. There was an inner glow to it—this rose would never die. Even if she hadn't given me that look, I would have been justifiably proud. Edge walked back to the fire with no further comment, but I saw the glances she threw my way when she thought I wasn't looking.

"I'm bushed," I said. "Let's stay here tonight and get an early start. I'll give you the news in the morning."

As we prepared for bed, I thought about how far we were from my office and my usual life. Looking up at the stars, twinkling in the black dome of the heavens, I wondered where this particular road would take me.

⁊

I woke up with a pleasant warmth down my left side. Edge had again moved, consciously or unconsciously, toward my warmth in the cold night. I gently brushed the hair out of her eyes with my hand. We should get going but, I wasn't going to be the one to break the mood, even if it was just my mood. I heard the crack of a twig from nearby. Edge was up with a knife in her hand before mine was fully from its sheath. I had a sneaking suspicion she'd been awake when I was making free with my hand a moment ago. Good thing common sense had dictated I stop at brushing her hair and not go for brushing her thigh. I might have found out what a pincushion feels like firsthand.

"I think it's an animal," I said. "I checked the area pretty thoroughly yesterday and we were alone for miles. We do have a party of about a dozen mercs following us though, so we'd better break camp."

Making her knife disappear again, Edge started getting her gear together. Tearing my eyes away from her lithe movements, I did the same. We started veering slightly to the west, to head more directly away from our pursuers. I also began to take more care in directing our path so as to avoid obvious indications of our passage. Edge picked up on these precautions rather quickly for a city girl. I guess caution had been second nature to her for a while in her profession.

The next few days passed in similar fashion. I would periodically check on the mercenaries, who seemed to have lost any hope of catching us with the death of their seeker. I was sure that would only last until they got word back to their employer, but that might not be for a while. Edge and I speculated that Francis must have had someone looking for her, or that any sudden departures from normal procedures by magicians in the city were being noted. Anyhow, I had thrown a light protective spell around us that would make us seem like a pair of traveling bears to the casual eye. Light because strong magic has a signature all its own that another practitioner would recognize. Bears because they would be common in this area at this time. Of course, we wouldn't fool a determined search, but for a hurried look, we would pass muster.

On the fifth day after my encounter with that other magician, we came to a small town. It was more a gathering of huts than a town. Its sole purpose was to serve as a meeting place for foresters and as a crossing place for the rapids that wound their way through the forest. As such, there was a muddy main street, with a tavern, a general store and an inn, along with a smattering of homes. I had dropped our disguise as we got closer to the dwellings. It wouldn't do to get shot for our skin.

As we trudged up to the tavern, a group of men showed some interest in Edge. The rotting wooden sign announced it as "The Reaver." A grim reaper with a bloody scythe completed the cheerful picture.

"Oy, mate, how much for her?" one of the men called out to me.

"She's not for sale," I replied, gaining a dirty look from Edge.

"Well, that's too bad," the man said with a grin, "cause I'm buying."

"You'd better shut your mouth, or I'll carve you a new arse," Edge said in a raspy drawl.

The man slowly unlimbered to his full height. He had looked perfectly normal sitting there, but he must have been at least six inches over my own six feet. And none of it was fat either.

"Don't give me no sass, missy," he rumbled, "or I'll put you over me knee and wallop you good." Stepping down to the street as he spoke, he picked a long staff up from where it was leaning against a hitching rail. Edge smiled sweetly and walked towards the man. "Now that's better," he laughed, looking back at his companions. His statement choked off into a high-pitched scream as Edge booted him in the balls. Without another glance at the squirming heap in the muddy street, Edge walked into the bar. I shrugged my shoulders and walked through the silent men behind her.

"I guess they'll forget all about us now," I said. "We'll just blend right in and when we're gone, we'll just slip right out of their minds." My heavy sarcasm slipped off her shoulders like water from an otter's skin.

"I don't like being talked about," was all she said. "Now let's get a beer and get out of here."

Well, I agreed with that part. Hiking sure is thirsty work. A noise at the door made us turn around. The giant had somehow got up, and he didn't look too pleased. Mud dripped off his nose to join the pile forming at his feet. His friends came in and spread out to watch the fun.

"Ye snuck one by me," he said, "but me eyes is open now! Come on, girlie."

Edge looked at me and said, "Order that beer. I'll be right back."

Well, nothing short of the end of the world could have made me turn around just then. And even that would be a near thing. Edge's casual air dropped from her as she glided closer to the far-from-jolly giant. I got the impression she was stalking him, even though he was the one now advancing. A seemingly casual flick of her hand swung his head left like he'd been hit with a sledgehammer. An equally casual return blow swung his head the other way. He shook it off, but I think he was having second thoughts right about now. His right hand swung out ponderously. If it had connected, I think Edge's head would have separated from the rest of her body. Slipping under the blow, she slammed the rigid ends of her fingertips up under his arm. He squealed like a bull becoming a steer. Left arm hanging like it was broken, he slowly withdrew.

Excited mutterings and the exchange of money told of some hot betting going on among the men. Faking a left to his face, Edge waited for his right arm to go up to block and gave it a similar treatment. If anything, his bellow was louder the second time. He did manage, however, to sweep his leg behind Edge's knees, causing her to fall backward. Turning the motion into a backflip, Edge's boot toe struck the man just behind the ear. As she completed her flip, a thunderous noise, as tables and chairs collapsed under the falling body, presaged a total silence.

I turned around and ordered two beers as if I hadn't just seen the second most amazing thing in my life. I'll leave the first to your imagination, but I'll tell you it involved a buxom but lonely widowed next-door neighbour when I was fourteen.

ও

After we downed our beers, we extricated ourselves from The Reaver with as minimal a fuss as possible. Edge got respectful nods from those locals still in the bar. A few others had dragged the downed giant outside. Of them, there was nary a glimpse. We still had a few good hours before darkness would force us to stop for the night, so I headed west after crossing the river. If anybody followed, looking for our whereabouts, hopefully they would get the wrong information. After a few miles, we once again turned north. I had been trapping some small animals as we went along, and we had restocked at the town. We were both in good shape, having toughened up the proper muscles. The air was bracing, the company great and the surroundings peaceful—something had to go wrong.

As we watched our campfire dying down to the embers, I listened to the wolves howling again. There was a peculiar note to the sound, something I'd never heard before. Edge had become used to the wolves, but even she seemed, well, on edge.

Making a decision, I turned to her, "Let's go!"

"Let's go where?" she replied.

Anywhere but here is what I wanted to say, but I didn't. Looking around, I spotted a slight rise with trees from which we could look down at our present location. "Over there," I pointed. Gathering up some branches, I stuffed our sleeping bags in such a way that it looked like we were sleeping there. Then, building up the fire, I followed Edge to the rise, covering over our tracks as I went. Something was nagging at my memory, but I couldn't quite place it.

Settling against a tree, I strung my bow and laid out some arrows in a neat row. The sound of the wolves was closer now. A note of excitement had crept into their voices. It sounded like they had struck our trail. Edge, catching my uneasiness, unslung her sword.

We didn't have long to wait. We counted an even dozen wolves bursting into the clearing in giant, silent leaps. There was something strange about them, besides their being twice as large as normal wolves. Their features were vaguely...human. Squinting to make sure, however, suddenly became unnecessary. The one nearest our sleeping bags stood up and blurred in the moonlight. A man stood there with a sword in his hands—neat trick. As his fellows gathered 'round, a few more changed. They, too, had swords. In a sudden fit of savagery, they lunged at the defenseless bags and started hacking away. When the trick I had played on him became obvious, the one who had changed first threw his head back and howled. The eerie wolf song coming from a human-seeming face was too much.

Nocking an arrow, I drew back, aimed and let go in a single motion. Not waiting to see if I had hit my target, I drew and fired another and another. I had used up my neat pile of arrows and there was silence in the clearing. There were two wolf bodies, five human bodies and the leader, caught in transformation, an arrow through his throat being gripped by wolf paws.

A quick count showed that we couldn't relax yet. Unless they had run off, which I wouldn't give odds on, I didn't want to be sitting here when the other four found us. I also didn't want to try to outsmart wolf senses in the dark.

"Up the tree," I directed Edge.

Keeping hold of her sword, she somehow managed to climb one-handed to the middle of the tree. Slinging my bow on my back, I joined her. Weaving some of the branches together and tying them, I prepared us a small nest. "I'll take first watch," I said. "I'll wake you up in a couple hours." The rest of my watch passed uneventfully, if uncomfortably. Waking Edge up, I thankfully drifted into oblivion.

I woke to the spray of hot blood on my cheek. Edge had spitted a wolf-man on her sword and was slashing at another with her belt-knife. Their features, close up, were predatory, with long, narrow jaws and sharp fangs. Their hair grew low on their foreheads and came to a point in the middle of their faces, just above their eyebrows. In the time it took me to see the first body fall, Edge had slashed the throat of one and opened up the belly of a third. I looked wildly around for the fourth. I felt the breeze of his rush and flattened myself to the branch I was on. But he wasn't after me. I guess he thought Edge was the dangerous one. Who am I kidding? She is the dangerous one.

Rolling onto her back, a rather dangerous maneuver on a branch fifty feet up in the air, Edge kicked out and up with both feet. The wolf, for he had transformed himself from start of leap to contact with Edge, caught both feet in his belly and was thrown out of the tree. Using the weight of the wolf on her feet to complete her roll, Edge was just in time to see the wolf impale himself on a nearby lightning-struck bole.

Watching him twitch with a self-satisfied air, Edge asked, "Are you OK?"

"Yeah, thanks for asking," I responded. "Why didn't you wake me sooner?"

"They would have heard," she said, "Besides, I couldn't let you have all the fun." Fun, she says. What have I got myself into.

༜

After cleaning off in a stream and retrieving what was left of our bedrolls, we headed north again. Somebody sure didn't like us going in this direction. Either that or I was on the worse run of luck I'd ever seen.

"We'd better plan what we want to do when we get closer to Francis," I said.

"Tonight," she replied shortly.

The rest of the day passed in a blur. Two hours of sleep after last night's excitement was not nearly enough. Edge also seemed worn-out and withdrawn. When we found a small clearing with a stream trickling through, we stopped by mutual consent. We could use the few hours left until daylight to devise a plan of attack.

"The first thing we need," she said, "is to get more information on where Francis is staying. That's your department. Then we have to list all his defenses and weaknesses. That's my department. Only then can we truly make a plan."

"It sounds good to me," I said, "but I'll need a good night's sleep before I'm willing to tackle whoever he's got warding that place."

"Let's go to bed then," she said with a slight smile. She couldn't mean...naw. As we snuggled under the remains of our sleeping gear, Edge gave me a quick kiss.

"What's that for?" I said with surprise tingeing my voice.

"Well, you did save our skins last night," she replied. After a moment's thought, I responded in kind. I held this kiss as long as I dared. "What was that for!" she said, a little breathlessly I was glad to note.

"Well," I said, "you saved us as well." Feeling a little smug, I drifted off to sleep.

❧

The morning dawned bright with promise. I was grateful to all this traveling time for allowing Edge and myself to draw closer together.

"Crystal," she said, once again surprising me.

"What?" I managed to get out.

"My name is Crystal, El," she replied. As I said...full of promise, this day.

We moved on. I was looking for a certain place, but I didn't know what it looked like. I only knew I'd know it when I saw it. Magic can be like that sometimes. Some places just draw you to them. And others repulse you. I'd never scientifically tested it, but I think like magic draws like magic. A thaumaturge is drawn to places where his type of magic abounds. A necromancer just naturally prefers the company of other necromancers. Besides, who else could stand the smell.

Anyway, after about an hour and a half of travel, I felt a tug off the path. Although it hadn't been there before, a few steps backward or forward did not lessen the need to change direction. I turned west and it intensified. Edge, ah, Crystal was looking at me in puzzlement. I didn't explain then, just shook my head and turned off the path. We travelled west for about an hour, and then veered northwest for another hour. We were reaching the foothills of the mountain range called Satan's Teeth. On the other side, somewhere, we would find Francis' stronghold.

The pull was stronger now. It led us up and among the ridges and valleys of the lower mountains. Finally, as darkness was fighting the sun for dominance over a blood red sky, we stood before a cave. We stooped to enter. I fashioned a light. The blue-green luminescence allowed us to see clearly. The cave stretched up and back, terminating in an abrupt vertical wall several feet back. Something about that wall drew my attention. As we got closer, I exclaimed, "It's man-made!"

"What is?" Crystal said.

"The wall," I said pointing. Examining each inch of the wall carefully, we found no sign of ingress. I summoned more light so we could go over it again in even finer detail. As the magic's presence made itself felt, a shadowy transparency appeared before us. Concentrating, I wrapped the strands of chaos around us in a filigreed cage. More like an extended suit of armor. Grasping Crystal's hand, I pressed forward boldly.

We merged with the wall. I felt the natural rock the wall was made of. We were that rock. I felt that I had been standing there for centuries, and would be for centuries more. I almost felt…a purpose. Then our momentum carried us through. I shudder to think what would have happened if I hadn't taken such a large step, or if the wall was thicker. We might have been there for years before another freed us—if it was possible.

Looking around, I heard a gasp. Crystal was staring with openmouthed amazement. The cave opened out into what must have been the majority of the mountain. Crystals of all colours and sizes shimmered in the artificial light offered by a glowing globe high up in the chamber. Glimmering sheets of fire paraded around, under and above us. I still felt that call. Taking Crystal's hand, I led us toward the globe. As we got closer, we could make out more details. It was faceted, like a diamond. Each face threw off a warm, yellow glow. It gave off a homey feeling, notwithstanding the flashiness of the rest of the chamber. We reached a final pile of crystals on which the globe rested. It began to pulsate as we grew nearer.

To my surprise, I recognized the beat—it was my own heart. A kind of keening began in my mind. A wave of feeling passed over me—of recognition, almost. I felt like I was about to meet a long-lost brother. Either my sense of perspective was being tampered with, or...yes, the globe was shrinking. The higher we climbed, the more rapidly it shrunk until it could have fit easily in the palm of my hand.

I sat down to ponder the situation. I didn't think the magic here was evil, but it was powerful, and dead was dead no matter what the intention. I let my awareness gradually expand and focused it on the globe. As my mind slipped into the "other" sight, I saw webs of power surrounding the object. Almost as if it *was* the mountain. I reached out again and gently reeled in the strands of the web, wrapping them around and around the globe in a pattern my subconscious dictated. I don't know how long it took, but finally it was done. There was a bright red flash as the last strand was fitted into the pattern and then nothing. I could still "see" the globe with my mind, but nothing but afterimage with my eyes. As I cupped my hand under it, there was a slight pop and it fell into my palm. It was warm and pulsed with a soft, internal light.

"You're finally out of it!" I turned to see Crystal coming out of her bedroll.

"What do you mean?" I said.

"I mean, you've been sitting there for about six hours. I've been unable to get closer than two paces. You had me worried," she added in an undertone.

"Sorry about that. I wasn't really conscious most of the time. Well, I'm not really sure what it is," I said, "but it's got a lot of power wrapped up in it. Let's go."

Calling the witchlight again, we retraced our steps to the wall. Before I could do anything, the globe in my hand pulsated and a doorway opened. It was as if the wall had become transparent in that section. We stepped through together. I headed back the way we had come, but Crystal stopped me.

"This way," she said.

"How do you know? I'm supposed to be the magician on this team."

"Oh, are we a team now?" she smiled back at me. That fleeting smile warmed my bones and made me willing to follow her anywhere. Was that the intention I wondered. Nah!

We followed some trail, known only to Crystal, for a good half hour. At the end of that time, we came to a totally featureless wall. Crystal continued walking straight toward it. "Um, don't you think we should stop *before* we bump our noses," I said.

She just looked at me and smiled, "If you can do it, I can do it."

"Yeah, but...magic..." I trailed off. She had quickened her steps, and we passed through where the wall should have been. Either a clever illusion or some pretty impressive magicking. Looking around, I snickered. "Pretty corny." There was a rock dead centre in the chamber. Smack in the middle of the rock was the protruding handle of a sword.

"Corny but also misleading," Crystal said. Making a wide circle around the rock, we approached it from the other side. Picking up a head-sized piece of rock, she threw it over to the other side. A brilliant spear of green light intersected the rock seconds after it hit the floor, turning it into dust.

"How did you know?" I asked.

"Just a feeling," she said smiling.

"Well, let me know if you have any more of those."

Crystal grabbed the hilt of the sword and pulled. It came loose as if from an oiled sheath. It was a magnificent construction. It also looked almost as tall as Crystal herself. "Now we can go?" she said.

We backtracked quickly. We decided to sleep in the cave that night as it was already dark. In fact, this was probably as good a place as any to look into Francis' whereabouts.

"I'll need a fire," I said. As we made camp and gathered firewood, I thought about what I'd have to do. Francis was only a few miles away over the hills. He would certainly have some strong wards in place. Still, there are ways.

༄

As I began meditating to clear my mind, I thought again of the crystal. As easy as that thought, the crystal appeared in my hand.

"Mbog!" I heard clearly in my mind.

"Huh?" I responded.

"Mbog," again, this time with a hint of amusement. "My name is Mbog."

I realized it was the crystal talking to me. I stared around wildly but, seeing the suspicious look on Crystal's face, and the way her sword hand was twitching, I quickly calmed myself. "Mbog?" I tried in my mind.

"You got it," was the smug reply.

"I'll talk to you later," I said. "Right now I've got work to do."

"Well, don't let me stop you," Crystal replied gruffly.

I realized I must have spoken out loud. "Not you," I said, "the crystal."

"I've never been called 'The Crystal' before," Crystal said.

"No, the rock. I'll explain later." With another strange look at me, she sat down and made herself comfortable.

The crystal felt strangely comforting cupped in my hands, so I left it there. I looked into and through the crystal, allowing my gaze to unfocus. I began to build a picture of Francis in my mind. I could feel his presence like a dull pain in the back of my head. I narrowed my awareness of him to a tiny sliver, smaller than a fragment of a fragment of glass. With this sliver of thought, I pierced the web of protective spells that were cast around his stronghold. The only problem with this mode of search was that, if discovered, my mind could be snapped as easily as that glass fragment.

I homed in on Francis. My awareness of his surroundings grew. He was in his castle, in the washroom and...oh, gross—he was naked. I pulled back my focus, first outside the room, then moving from room to room, building up a mental map of his defenses. A short hour later, I withdrew. Looking over at Crystal, I saw that she was asleep. I cuddled up next to her to get a few winks myself. I hoped the delectable aroma I smelled was some sort of scent. Otherwise, my wild imagination might keep me up, so to speak.

The next morning the sun treated us to a light show. I felt invigorated. We were coming to the end of our quest. I hoped that if we made it through alive, I would have a chance of some sort of life with Crystal. But first things first.

"Crystal," I said, kneeling over her. "Take that knife away from my throat, it's time to get up." God, but she could move fast. "I have a map of the grounds. I want to pass it to you mentally, so you'll know all I know."

"How are you going to do that?" she said suspiciously.

"Just trust me," I said. Putting my hand behind her neck and the other on her forehead—not strictly necessary, just enjoyable—I stared into her eyes. Slipping slightly into trance, I imagined the map in my head as a piece of paper. I carefully folded it and slipped it into her mind. There is no other way to explain. I know,

I've tried. I "watched" as she unfolded it and then slipped out of the light trance. I kissed her lightly on the lips.

"Is that the way you do it with men also?" she said mischievously.

Ignoring her crack, I asked, "Got it?"

"Yes," she said wonderingly, "just as if I'd drawn it myself."

"OK, let's move out."

As we covered the last few miles to the castle, I rehearsed some quick spells so I could throw them later without thought. As we crested the last hill, the valley opened out before us. Francis' castle was large and heavily fortified. Luckily, we shouldn't have to fight our way in. I turned to Crystal, "What I'm going to do now is turn us into birds. Just be careful to remember you're human. You tend to start to like the looks of worms and such. Forget about it—we eat later."

I was touched to see the trust she put in me. No questions were asked. No "What happens if you die, am I stuck as a bird?" I concentrated: Let's see...robins. No, sparrows. I don't really think anyone would shoot at us, but you never know. I formed the images in my mind and imposed my picture on present reality. Doing two people was trickier than one normally, but felt easier today. There was a helpful surge of power from the location of the crystal around my neck and we were airborne. Some beginners find it necessary to practice in the forms they assumed before they were proficient. I, however, was good enough to build that skill in magically.

As we winged our way towards the upstairs windows, we saw the glint of men patrolling the grounds. They were wearing armor and carrying halberds. We slipped into the castle proper and almost lost right there as a cat launched itself at what it obviously thought was dinner. As we morphed back into our proper forms, the cat screeched and disappeared around the corner. I think the birds in this area were safe, for a little while anyway.

"That was fun," Crystal said. Whirling suddenly, her hand blurred towards her sword and the embrasure was filled with a luminous blue light. I looked down at the head of a guard that had previously been resting on a very muscular pair of shoulders. There wasn't even any blood. Then I looked incredulously at the blazing sword in Crystal's hand. It was the one from the cave.

Picking my jaw up off the floor, I said "Well you'd better turn it off unless you want the whole castle to know we're here."

"I don't know how," she replied as the light went out. I was looking at plain metal again. Oh well, stranger things have happened. I don't know where, but I'm sure they have.

I concentrated briefly, and a small globe of pulsating yellow light appeared in my hand. Concentrating on Francis again, I let it go. It went off down the corridor and stopped at the second door, then winked out. "Shall we?" I asked.

As I burst the door in with a short flare of pure energy, we could see three people inside. One was wearing a black cloak and a tall hat, both covered in mystic symbols. Corny as hell, but obviously Francis' master magician. The other had the supple movements of a hunting cat and had a sword halfway out of its sheath. Chief bodyguard, I would assume. And the third man, with the yellow puddle appearing at his feet—that was Francis. A blur that was Crystal went by on my left and a blast of magical energy brought me out of my musings.

With the afterimage of the blast seared into my retinas, I allowed my sight to shift so I could see the magical energies directly. A second and third blast also fizzled on my defensive shields. Time to make a nuisance of myself. I like to be creative. Pure blasts of energy are so blasé. I pictured a large bear trap below my opponent, and pictured the jaws snapping shut. My imagination created a corresponding image in the magical energies surrounding my enemy. With a surprised squeak, he managed to erect a shield that prevented the separation of body and soul. Some mages are unprepared for such gruesome images. It can give a fellow a distinct advantage.

Without allowing him time to regroup, a large snake with blazing red eyes appeared before him. The jaws opened wider than his head as the muscular coils snapped the body forward. At the last minute, a large mongoose appeared out of nowhere and bit the snake behind the neck. Both animals struggled, then flared and fizzled out. He was recovering too quickly. Time for a strategy change. Concentrating on the floor underneath his feet, I dissolved the stone, plummeting him some twenty-five feet into the room below. A satisfying crack signalled at least one broken leg. Following him somewhat less precipitously, I left the two swords raising sparks off each other.

The pain must have been considerable, but another blast of energy singed my hair and exploded out the wall at my back. If the other forces at the castle didn't know about us before, they certainly did now. Changing tactics again, I formed a bar of pure energy, like a staff, in my hands. Swinging it at his head, I forced him to duck...into the toe of my boot. The force of the blow flung him against the wall. I began beating at his head and shoulders with my mystic staff, forcing him to expend energy in protecting himself. Black flickers in the surface of his shield signalled that the pain of his injuries was sapping his strength. As he was expecting me to continue with my magical attack, I threw the bar at his head with one hand and slid my dirk between his ribs with the other. As a friend of mine once said, his last words in fact, "It's hard to think with a knife in your ribs." One last burst of energy ensured that he wouldn't be healing himself and coming after me for more.

Leaving the sizzling pile of what had once been human behind, I levitated cautiously back through the hole in the ceiling. I was horrified to catch a glimpse of Francis' knife whirling lazily through the air on a direct path to Crystal's back. A blue flare from her sword coursed over her body, covering her from head to toe in shimmering flame. The knife bounced off this nimbus, nearly impaling Francis in the process. I could see her opponent desperately blocking her lightning slashes to his head and arms. Numerous slashes in his breeches and jerkin attested that he was only doing a barely adequate job. As he responded to a feint with her sword, Crystal's other hand drove her knife into his ribs. I knew we were made for each other, we even thought alike.

Francis, seeing which way the wind had blown, made a beeline for the doorway where he confronted a large lion. Staggering backwards into the room, he fell on his rather large behind.

"What do you want to do with him?" I asked.

"Roast him in oil, cut off his fingers and toes, pluck out his eyes, and then get really nasty," Crystal replied.

At that point Francis fainted. When we revived him with a solid boot to the gut, he tried to bribe his way out of the predicament he was in.

"Won't wash," I said, "I can sign your name to a will giving me all your worldly goods or make you sign—before or after you're dead."

Crystal looked at me, "What's the worst way you can kill him?"

"Name your choice," I replied, "but the best way to punish him is to keep him alive. I know a certain port where ships sail with prostitutes for the mines."

"But they only take women!" Crystal said.

"If I can make us into birds, I think I can handle making him a woman."

Crystal smiled. "I know one woman who's looking forward to a little handling from you as soon as we get rid of him."

# Daddy's Girl
*By Abegail Dagdag*

It was a snow day, that day. Some things had happened, and no one knew what exactly had happened, or even why. No one except three people.

## Emily Fennings, Victim

I've watched tons of movies involving break-ins, stabbings and those kinds of things. But I never thought that I would ever be in a situation like that.

One Friday morning the familiar sound of my alarm clock woke me up to get ready for school. I opened my window a little to let in some air. As I felt the cold air surround me, I couldn't help but notice all the snow covering the neighborhood. I expected it to be a chilly, snow-less winter day. I ran downstairs to check the news to see whether it was going to be a snow day, and it was.

I peeked outside the window beside the front door to see if I would have to shovel later that day, or maybe get someone to do it for me. But the amount of snow in my driveway wasn't what caught my attention. It was those holes near my backyard door, like foot prints, only deeper. I shivered slightly and remembered that I had left my window open upstairs.

I threw down a quick bowl of cereal and a glass of orange juice to take up to my room. When I got to my room, I put down my breakfast, turned on the computer, closed my window and took a pair of comfy sweats out of the drawer to change into. I went in the bathroom to freshen up and to change. Just when I got back to my room, I saw all three windows widely open. I didn't hear anything, I thought, and I remember closing the window. I closed them anyway, thinking I just imagined closing them, not realizing that something might be wrong.

I sat down and turned to my breakfast beside the computer. Just then, I heard the loud clattering of knives, forks and spoons.

The sound had come from the kitchen. Is someone else in the house, I wondered, and shuddered at the thought. Immediately, I realized that maybe someone had come through the window that I left open earlier. I stood up quickly, and as I approached the window, I slipped and fell on the floor.

"What the…"

Then I saw it. My floor was covered in water and slush. My eyes flashed to the window. More slush and water. I picked myself up and grabbed the cordless phone. As I pressed the Talk button I saw the figure. A tall dark figure was standing beside the stairs, its head turning in my direction.

The line was dead. But I could hear the phone downstairs ringing. I dropped the phone and quickly ran to the nearest window, as the dark figure walked slowly in the hallway and into my room.

I panicked. I wasn't looking at what I was putting my hands on because my eyes were focused on the nearing figure. Then something caught my attention, a shining pointed thing the person was holding in their left hand—a knife.

I took one quick glance at the thing I grabbed and pulled it. I scraped my right arm along the edge of the window as I stuck my head out, trying to escape through the window in my room. Struggling as I was, I managed to pull my body, just somewhere below my shoulders, out of the window.

Over the pain of my arm, I felt the person behind me stab the middle of my back with the knife. That was the last thing I remember, just before falling from my second-floor window.

**Nadine Patsburg, Witness**

At 6 o'clock in the morning, I was already up and ready for school. It was a Friday, almost the weekend, something I always looked forward to. Since school wasn't going to start for about another two and a half hours, I decided that I would watch some TV.

The ringing of the phone had woken me up. I hadn't even noticed that I had fallen asleep on the couch, with the TV still on. I glanced at the clock, which told me that it was already 7 o'clock; I had slept for an hour on the couch. My mother had just called and left a message on the answering machine. I'll call her later, I said to myself. I changed the channel to the news. The news reporters had just announced that the high school I went to was closed because of all the snow covering the roads. (Most kids in my school drive). I guess it's a snow day then, I thought. I went upstairs into my room to change back into my pajamas. I lay back down on my bed, trying to sleep again. But after a few minutes, I gave up.

I went to my phone, calling up my best friend, Emily. Emily lives right across from my house, but we liked to call instead of going over to each other's house just to tell the other something. I picked up my phone and dialed her number, but no one answered. I tried again, still nothing. I wondered what had happened to her. I took out my binoculars and looked at her bedroom window.

From where I was standing, I saw that her back was to the window. I could tell that she was trying to open it, but it looked as if she was having trouble doing so. She looked at the bottom of the window very quickly, and then turned her head away from it.

Finally, she managed to open it and stick her hands and shoulders out, just before I noticed the figure behind her. The figure raised its left hand, holding something pointed, which it jabbed into her back.

"No!" I screamed.

As I dropped my binoculars in shock, I watched my best friend fall out of her second-floor window and into the snow in her driveway. I managed to pick up my phone again, still in shock, to call 911.

"911, what's your emergency?"

"My best friend just fell out of her window and I think she's unconscious…and I think someone stabbed her in her back…she lives in 9826 Maple Street, please hurry."

The person on the line was asking me questions, but I was just too preoccupied as I stared at Emily's body to pay any attention to what she was saying. Luckily, I answered them without realizing I even did.

I grabbed my jacket off the rack, put on my winter boots and rushed out the door to help Emily. She had been stabbed in her back, and she was bleeding from her right arm and from her back.

The EMS came and took her to the hospital. I couldn't go with her just yet because I had to tell the police what I had witnessed. Emily's safe now, I kept telling myself, but I just had to be with her. And when I was allowed to go see her, she was still sleeping, so I just sat on the couch in the room and drifted off to sleep without even knowing it.

## The Suspect

Thursday afternoon, the phone rang while I was watching TV.

"Answer the damn phone, Rosa! I'm trying to watch some TV here!" I shouted to Rosa that she should answer it, since I wasn't planning to. The ringing stopped immediately, and the squealing began. Rosa was squealing on the phone for some reason. Why? I picked up the receiver of the phone that was on the table beside me, pressed the Talk button and put it to my ear.

"Honey, engaged! Wow!" Rosa squealed.

"Don't tell him though…well, at least not now," Emily said.

Engaged? Emily? Emily is engaged and I am not to be informed about it? Anger spread through my body.

"Of course I won't honey, we don't want him to lose his temper…I'm so happy for you!" Rosa said. She continued on, "You know, he has had some difficulties in controlling it for quite a while now, so…"

I felt my face turn red as she said this. I didn't want to hear any more about it. As fury filled me, I kept trying to understand what I had just heard. It couldn't be true. Emily is only eighteen, she can't get married yet. She's too young. So what if she has her own house? So what if she has a job and is making good money? She can't! She just can't!

After an awkward dinner, I quickly cleaned myself and went to lie down in bed, but didn't sleep immediately. I was putting together a plan that would convince Emily that she can't marry anyone just yet. After about two hours of brainstorming, I still hadn't come up with anything.

I know Emily's routine in the morning, and one of the things she always does after she wakes up is open her upstairs window to let in some cool air. Then she goes downstairs to check the news. When she's downstairs, I'll sneak up her window and…I couldn't think of anything else, so I decided that I would just go with the flow the following morning. I fell asleep, imagining what I was to do the next day.

I woke up early to shovel the driveway and to leave the house even before the traffic started. When I got to her house, I parked the car on the corner of the street so that she wouldn't know I was in her neighborhood. I was just in time. I saw her hand was sticking out the window. I knew she kept a short ladder in her backyard, so I took it to help me get up the downspout, and from there, maybe I could climb my way up to her open window.

It wasn't very easy, but luckily I made it up to her room. But I accidentally unplugged the telephone line as I was walking towards her bedroom door. That entire "climbing up her window exercise" was just too much for a man my age, and it made me feel really hot. So I opened all the windows in her room to let in cold air to cool me down. I then hid in the linen closet until she went into the bathroom. As she closed the bathroom door, I opened the linen closet door and made my way downstairs without making noise.

I went into the kitchen and looked around. There was a picture of Emily and a boy I recognized, Frankie. They were both smiling. It was stuck on the fridge door with a magnet. There was a hand-drawn heart around both of them, and an arrow pointing at the boy with a label saying "My Dearest Fiancé."

The same fury ran through me again, just like last night. Without even thinking what I was doing, I grabbed a handful of kitchen utensils from one of the drawers and took out the longest, most pointed knife of all; I marched up the stairs. I heard a loud thud coming from Emily's room. I turned my head in the direction of her room and saw her drop her cordless phone and run to the window that was behind her.

As I entered her room, she was already looking in my direction, with horror in her eyes. She turned around for about a fraction of a second to open the window. She stuck out her limbs as I released my anger by jabbing the knife that I held with all my power into her back.

As I watched her fall from her window, I started to come to my senses. I couldn't believe that I had just done something I will regret for the rest of my life. I had just stabbed my one, and only, lovely daughter, Emily.

For more information and/or to request a personalized story, contact

## THE INSPIRATION ROOM
at
TeachtheChildrennow@yahoo.ca